DK BACKPACK BOOKS

1,001 FACTS ABOUT
ANCIENT EGYPT

MUMMIFIED
HEAD

ANUBIS, THE JACKAL
GOD OF EMBALMING

FOOT CASE FROM
A MUMMY

OUTER AND INNER
MUMMY CASES

DK BACKPACK BOOKS

1,001 FACTS ABOUT
ANCIENT EGYPT

Written by SCOTT STEEDMAN
with additional material by MARILYN INGLIS

GODDESS
HATHOR

LOTUS FLOWER
DRINKING CUP

SPHINX
SCULPTURE

A DK Publishing Book

LONDON, NEW YORK, MUNICH,
MELBOURNE, and DELHI

Project editor Clare Lister
Senior designer Adrienne Hutchinson
Senior editorial coordinator Camilla Hallinan
Senior design coordinator Sophia M. Tampakopoulos Turner
DTP designer Jill Bunyan
Category publisher Sue Grabham
Production Linda Dare
With thanks to the original team
Project editor Linda White
Art editor Ann Cannings
Senior editor Hazel Egerton
Senior art editor Jacquie Gulliver
Editorial consultant Angela Thomas
Picture research Giselle Harvey
Additional material created by Book Creation Services
First American Edition, 2003
05 10 9 8 7 6 5 4 3 2

Published in the United States by DK Publishing, Inc.
375 Hudson Street, New York, New York 10014

A catalog record for this book is available from the Library of Congress.

ISBN-13: 978-0-7894-9040-7
ISBN-10: 0-7894-9040-4

Color reproduction by Colourscan, Singapore
Printed and bound in Singapore by Star Standard

See our complete product line at
www.dk.com

CONTENTS

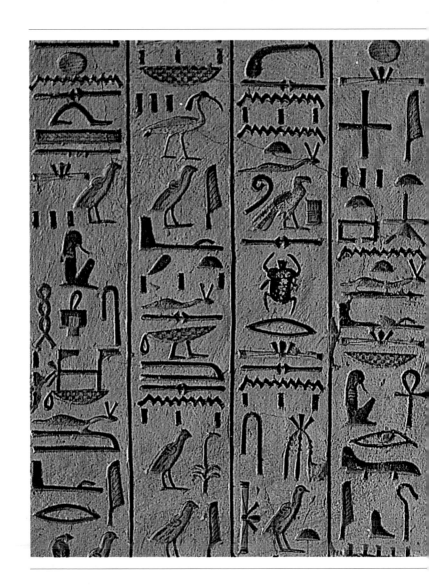

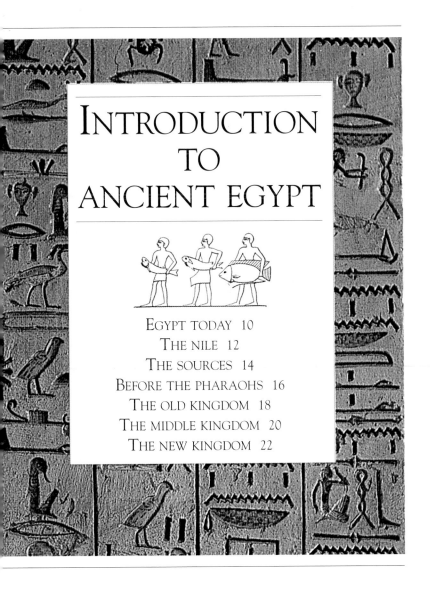

INTRODUCTION TO ANCIENT EGYPT

EGYPT TODAY

THE NILE RIVER and the Sahara Desert dominate Egypt. Until recently, the Nile flooded every year, bringing fertile black soil to the farmland on its banks. The ancient Egyptians called this lush strip the "black land," the land of life. The scorching desert was the "red land," the land of death.

CAIRO
Egypt's capital, Cairo, is the largest city in Africa, with a population of over 11 million. It was founded by Muslims in A.D. 969, more than a thousand years after the last pharaoh.

SAILING ON THE NILE
The Nile is the longest river in the world, flowing 4,145 miles (6,670 km) from the highlands of East Africa to the Mediterranean Sea.

FACTS ABOUT EGYPT

• The Sahara is the world's largest desert.

• Egypt is Africa's second biggest country (population: 55 million).

• Egypt has been a Muslim country since A.D. 642.

• The Aswan High Dam, built in 1969–70, ended the annual floods.

PYRAMIDS AND SPHINX
These famous monuments are both in Giza, on the outskirts of Cairo. They were built 4,500 years ago, during the period known as the Old Kingdom.

QUEEN HATSHEPSUT'S TEMPLE
Millions of tourists come to
Egypt every year to visit its great
monuments and museums. This
is Queen Hatshepsut's mortuary
temple at Deir el-Bahri on the
west bank of the Nile near Luxor.

KING'S COFFIN
The Egyptians had
elaborate beliefs
about life after
death. Pharaohs
and the elite were
mummified and
buried with a
wealth of treasure
in decorated
tombs. These are
a rich source of
information on
ancient life.

MODERN MAP WITH OLD SITES
Buildups of silt in the north
has altered Egypt's coastline.
Other changes are the Suez
Canal and the Aswan Dam.

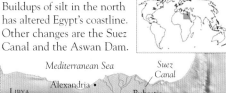

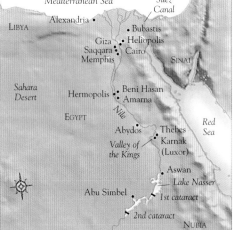

THE NILE

EGYPT HAS BEEN CALLED "the Gift of the Nile." All the water for drinking, bathing, and watering crops came from the great river. The Nile was also Egypt's main highway. The dominant wind blew from north to south, so boats could float downstream with the current or sail upstream against it.

ANCIENT WAYS
Egyptians still grow crops and raise livestock on the banks of the Nile, as they have been doing for more than 7,000 years.

TOMB MODEL FOR USE IN THE AFTERLIFE

FISHING NET

Prow

FISH HOOKS

Man rowing

Sun canopy

Steersman

Steering oar

BOAT
A text from c.1100 B.C. records "Merchants sail up and downstream, eager to convey goods from one place to another and to supply whatever is needed anywhere."

HUNTING AND FISHING
The Nile teemed with life. Men hunted birds in the marshes and caught fish with nets or hooks and lines. Children were taught to be afraid of crocodiles and hippos, which could overturn boats.

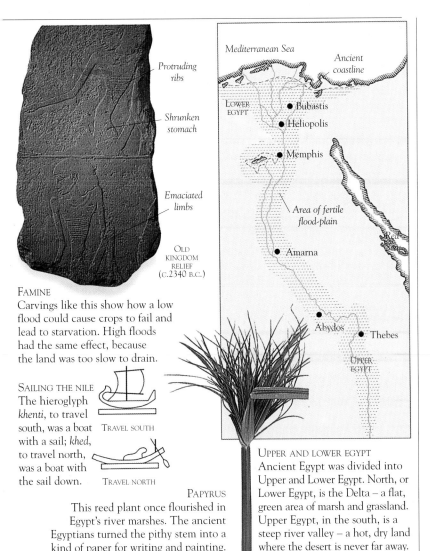

Mediterranean Sea

Ancient coastline

LOWER EGYPT

● Bubastis

● Heliopolis

● Memphis

Area of fertile flood-plain

Red Sea

● Amarna

Abydos ● ● Thebes

UPPER EGYPT

Protruding ribs

Shrunken stomach

Emaciated limbs

OLD KINGDOM RELIEF (C.2340 B.C.)

FAMINE
Carvings like this show how a low flood could cause crops to fail and lead to starvation. High floods had the same effect, because the land was too slow to drain.

SAILING THE NILE
The hieroglyph *khenti*, to travel south, was a boat with a sail; *khed*, to travel north, was a boat with the sail down.

TRAVEL SOUTH

TRAVEL NORTH

PAPYRUS
This reed plant once flourished in Egypt's river marshes. The ancient Egyptians turned the pithy stem into a kind of paper for writing and painting.

UPPER AND LOWER EGYPT
Ancient Egypt was divided into Upper and Lower Egypt. North, or Lower Egypt, is the Delta – a flat, green area of marsh and grassland. Upper Egypt, in the south, is a steep river valley – a hot, dry land where the desert is never far away.

13

THE SOURCES

OUR KNOWLEDGE of ancient Egypt comes from buildings, objects, and writings. Many disappeared over the centuries. Thieves stole treasures, and the desert sands invaded temples and tombs. But a hot, dry climate preserved monuments well. Egyptologists study these, and other sources, for clues to Egypt's past.

MYSTERIOUS LAND
Sources can never give a complete picture of the past. This is the Queen of Punt, a land somewhere to the south. We still do not know exactly where.

GUTENBERG BIBLE
Jews and Christians learned about Egypt from the Old Testament of the Bible (the Jewish Torah). It tells the story of the Jews' exile in Egypt, where many worked as slaves for the pharaoh.

THE FIRST PRINTED BIBLE

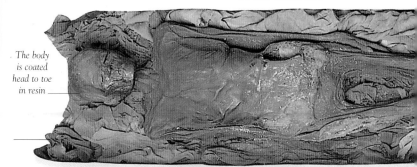

The body is coated head to toe in resin

NAPOLEON IN EGYPT

When the French general Napoleon invaded Egypt in 1798, he brought a team of scholars and artists who made detailed studies of temples, tombs, and mummies. This sparked off the West's fascination with Egypt.

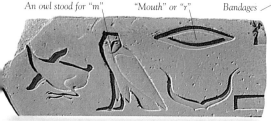

An owl stood for "m"   *"Mouth" or "r"*   *Bandages*

HIEROGLYPHS

Egyptian monuments, statues, and other artifacts are covered in hieroglyphs, a type of picture-writing. In 1822, French linguist Champollion discovered how to read them and opened up a huge new source of information.

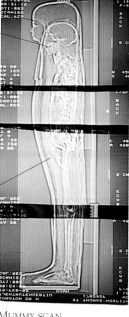

Mummy case
Skeleton

Bandages

MUMMY SCAN

During the 19th century, mummies were unwrapped, often as public events. This was destructive and disrespectful. Now modern scanners can create 3-D X-ray images of a mummy.

Linen bandages

MUMMIFICATION

The Egyptians went to incredible lengths to preserve their bodies for eternity. Mummies give us all sorts of information about health, diet, and disease. This woman's teeth were worn down by a lifetime of chewing coarse bread. We can even identify the plant oils used to preserve her skin.

15

BEFORE THE PHARAOHS

SETTLERS BEGAN TO FARM the Nile
Valley in about 5000 B.C. They
prospered and eventually formed
two kingdoms, Upper Egypt
and Lower Egypt. These early
Egyptians believed in life after
death. They buried their
dead in sand graves with
items for the next life.

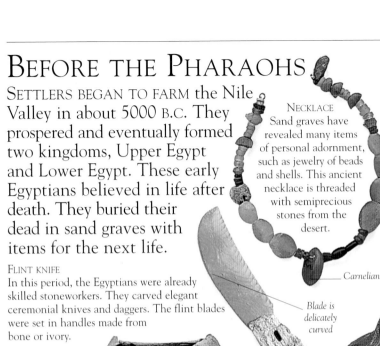

NECKLACE
Sand graves have
revealed many items
of personal adornment,
such as jewelry of beads
and shells. This ancient
necklace is threaded
with semiprecious
stones from the
desert.

Carnelian

FLINT KNIFE
In this period, the Egyptians were already
skilled stoneworkers. They carved elegant
ceremonial knives and daggers. The flint blades
were set in handles made from
bone or ivory.

Blade is
delicately
curved

Roofs
were
thatched

Wattle and
daub walls

Wood
beams above
doors and windows

Toenail

MODEL HOUSE FROM GRAVE
The time before the pharaohs is known as the
Predynastic period (5000–3100 B.C.). In Upper
Egypt, farmers lived in small villages on the high
ground above the Nile, in houses like this one.

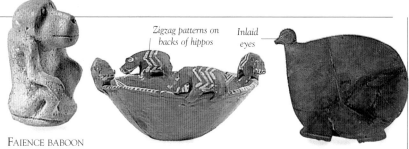

FAIENCE BABOON
This is made from a glazed earthenware called faience, which first appeared in Egypt during this period.

Zigzag patterns on backs of hippos

Inlaid eyes

HIPPO BOWL
Early potters used Nile silt and clay. The river was also a source of inspiration. This bowl is decorated with hippos.

SHEEP SHAPE
This sheep-shaped stone palette was for grinding makeup. Others are in the form of hippos, turtles, and falcons. These mysterious objects probably had a magical purpose as well.

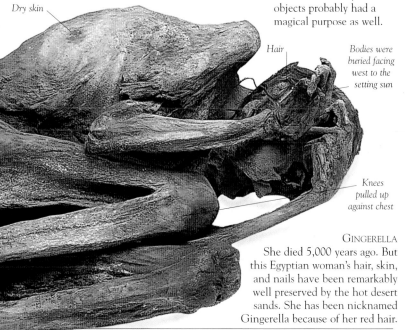

Dry skin

Hair

Bodies were buried facing west to the setting sun

Knees pulled up against chest

GINGERELLA
She died 5,000 years ago. But this Egyptian woman's hair, skin, and nails have been remarkably well preserved by the hot desert sands. She has been nicknamed Gingerella because of her red hair.

THE OLD KINGDOM

EGYPT WAS UNIFIED for the first time in about 3100 B.C., more than 400 years before the start of the Old Kingdom, or "Pyramid Age." Under the stable rule of powerful pharaohs, the country's economy and culture flourished. Art and architecture reached a peak with the building of the great pyramids at Giza.

DOUBLE CROWN
As a symbol of his power, the pharaoh wore the *pschent* or double crown. This combined the White Crown, worn by the kings of Upper Egypt, and the Red Crown of Lower Egypt's kings.

RULER OF TWO LANDS
The union of Egypt is shown here by the entwined lotus (symbol of Upper Egypt) and papyrus (Lower Egypt). One of the pharaoh's official titles was "Ruler of the Two Lands."

Painted limestone

Papyrus plant

Lotus

KING KHAFRA'S THRONE (DETAIL)

ROYAL COUPLE
These beautiful statues are Prince Rahotep and his wife Nofret. They were found near the pyramid of his father, King Sneferu. The statues are so lifelike it is hard to believe they are 4,600 years old. The eyes are rock crystal, with irises of purple amethyst.

FIRST PHARAOH?
Legend tells that
Egypt was united
by Menes, a king
from Upper Egypt
who conquered
the north. Experts
believe he may be
King Narmer (here
wearing the White
Crown). On the other
side of this palette, he
wears the Red Crown.

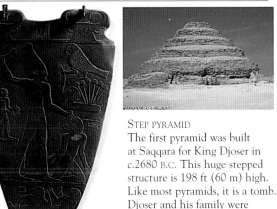

NARMER'S
PALETTE

King
Narmer

KHUFU
SMITES
ENEMY
CHIEF

MIGHTY KINGS
Kings Khufu, Khafra, and
Menkaura, builders of the
Pyramids of Giza, were
among the most powerful.
They must have directed
Egypt's entire economy
into building their tombs.

GOD-KING
The Egyptians believed
that the pharaoh was the
son of the sun god Ra. The
king was also associated with the
sky god, Horus, seen here as a
falcon protecting Khafra.

STEP PYRAMID
The first pyramid was built
at Saqqara for King Djoser in
c.2680 B.C. This huge stepped
structure is 198 ft (60 m) high.
Like most pyramids, it is a tomb.
Djoser and his family were
buried in chambers far beneath.

Sky god,
Horus

Nemes
headdress

Royal beard

THE MIDDLE KINGDOM

THE OLD KINGDOM COLLAPSED in about 2160 B.C., and Egypt was rocked by war and chaos. It was eventually reunited by Mentuhotep, who founded the Middle Kingdom in 2040 B.C. Peace and prosperity returned. Strong pharaohs strengthened government and foreign trade, and Egypt invaded Libya and Nubia. Art revived, and pyramids were built again.

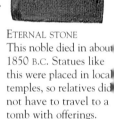

SENUSRET I
This dynamic king took the throne after sharing it for ten years with his father, Amenemhat I. Senusret I fought the Libyans and Nubians and built many grand temples. The earliest known literary texts were written in his court.

ETERNAL STONE
This noble died in about 1850 B.C. Statues like this were placed in local temples, so relatives did not have to travel to a tomb with offerings.

Spells cover coffin inside and out

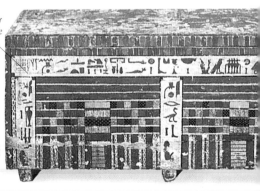

MUMMY CASE
Middle Kingdom coffins were painted with magical spells to help the soul on its journey through the underworld to the next life. During the Old Kingdom, these spells – known as the Pyramid texts – had been carved in royal tombs.

AMENEMHAT III
During his long and peaceful reign (1854–1808 B.C.), this powerful pharaoh built temples, border forts, two pyramids, and undertook a land reclamation scheme.

BLACK PYRAMID
This is the first pyramid of Amenemhat III, which he built at Dahshur. Like all Middle Kingdom pyramids, the core is of mud bricks rather than stone. These have collapsed in a shapeless heap.

UNDER THE BLACK PYRAMID
Kings built mazes of false passages and hidden doors to try to conceal their burial chambers from robbers. It did not work. The Middle Kingdom collapsed in 1750 B.C., and all the pyramids were looted during the chaos that followed.

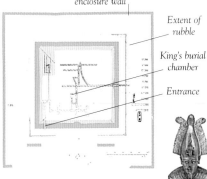

Pyramid enclosure wall

Extent of rubble

King's burial chamber

Entrance

False eyes allow mummy to "see" out

OSIRIS

GOD OF THE DEAD
The worship of Osiris, god of death and rebirth, spread across Egypt in the Middle Kingdom. He offered all Egyptians, not just those close to the pharaoh, the hope of an afterlife.

21

THE NEW KINGDOM

THE GREATEST PERIOD of Egypt's history was the New Kingdom (c.1550–1086 B.C.). Warrior kings, such as Ahmose I and Thutmose III, expanded the empire into Nubia, Libya, and the Middle East. Many temples were built, and pharaohs were buried in painted tombs in the Valley of the Kings.

WAR CROWN
The pharaoh's new image was as a war leader. He adopted the Blue Crown, or war helmet, and was seen as a living form of a warrior god.

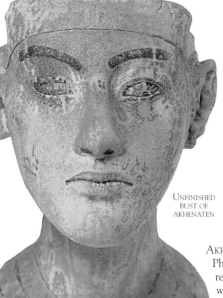

UNFINISHED BUST OF AKHENATEN

RAMSES THE GREAT
In his 67 years on the throne, Ramses II built more monuments than any other pharaoh. This is the massive rock-cut temple of Abu Simbel. The four statues of Ramses II are each 65 ft (20 m) high.

AKHENATEN, HERETIC PHARAOH
Pharaoh Amenhotep IV introduced a new religion, the first in history based on the worship of one god (the Aten). He even changed his name to Akhen*aten*. After his death, his name was scorned, his city abandoned, and the gods were reinstated.

22

WAR CHARIOT
To expel Asian invaders,
the first pharaohs of
the New Kingdom built an
efficient army. This included corps of war
chariots, copied from the Asian enemy.

TOMB OF SENNEDJEM (DEIR EL-MEDINA)
The Egyptians gave up on pyramid tombs, which were
too easy to find and rob. Instead, they were buried in
tombs cut deep into the rock in barren spots like the
Valley of the Kings and the Valley of the Queens.

MASS GLASS
Factories, mass-producing
colorful glass vessels, were
set up near many palaces.
Glass was also cast to
decorate jewelry, furniture,
and even mummy cases.

TUTANKHAMUN'S SECOND COFFIN
The tombs in the Valley of the Kings were robbed long ago.
The only one found intact belonged to an obscure boy-king
called Tutankhamun. The glittering treasures
inside amazed the world.

*Colored
glass*

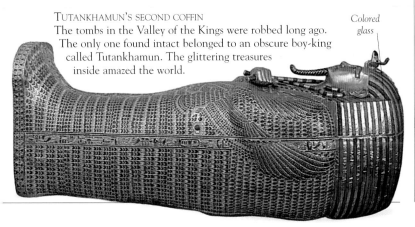

EGYPTIAN SOCIETY

THE PEOPLE OF EGYPT

AT THE TOP of Egyptian society was the pharaoh. He commanded the army and ruled the country through a network of nobles, officials, and scribes. Skillful craftsworkers were kept busy building and decorating temples and tombs. But most Egyptians were peasants who worked the land.

AT THE PHARAOH'S SIDE
In life as in death, the king was surrounded by his nobles. This noble's tomb is in the shadow of King Khufu's Pyramid.

Tomb of Seshemnufer

SERVANT GIRL
Many women worked as servants in the houses of the rich. This wooden palette is in the shape of a serving girl, carrying a large pot on one shoulder. It is a makeup container; the top slides open and closed.

A KEEPER OF RECORDS
Scribes were important because they were among the few who could read and write. They recorded many details of everyday life.

FACTS ABOUT PEOPLE

• A massive tomb recently discovered in the Valley of the Kings (1995) shows that it contains at least some of Ramses II's many sons.

• When the pharaoh praised one man's work, the man died of shock.

HARVEST SCENE
Farming life followed the seasons. As soon as the summer's crop was ripe, farmers rushed to harvest it before the Nile flooded the land again. These oxen are treading the grain.

OFFICIAL
The state was highly bureaucratic. Every town had officials. These civil servants collected taxes, regulated businesses, and organized loans and marriage contracts.

CRAFTSWORKERS
Most craftsworkers were employed in workshops run by royal palaces or temples. This carpenter is building a ship for a wealthy patron.

MUSICIAN
The Egyptians believed in enjoying life. Dancers and musicians performed at the royal courts and at private dinner parties. They also entertained the bustling crowds during festivals and celebrations.

KING AND CAPTIVE
The pharaoh was seen as a living god. He led in battle and protected Egypt from famine, disease, and chaos. This is symbolized by this statue of pharaoh Ramses IV gripping a captive enemy.

PEASANTS AND SERVANTS

THE VAST MAJORITY of ancient Egyptians were peasant farmers. They worked in the fields by the Nile, channeling the floodwaters and planting and harvesting crops. Many others worked as servants or laborers. Few of them could read or write. But they enjoyed more freedom than slaves, who were rare.

FOREIGN SLAVES
Slaves were never an important part of Egyptian society and were rare until the New Kingdom. Most slaves were foreigners, captured during Egypt's wars abroad. Here, a scribe registers foreign captives.

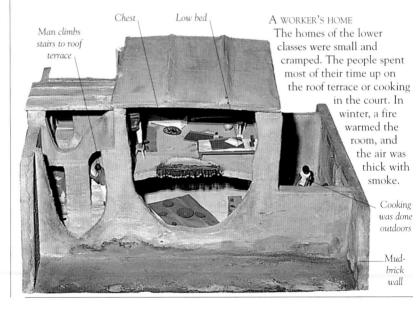

Chest

Low bed

Man climbs stairs to roof terrace

A WORKER'S HOME
The homes of the lower classes were small and cramped. The people spent most of their time up on the roof terrace or cooking in the court. In winter, a fire warmed the room, and the air was thick with smoke.

Cooking was done outdoors

Mud-brick wall

A BEATING

Peasants who did not pay their taxes were beaten. More serious criminals were whipped or had their noses cut off and then sent to the mines of Sinai or Nubia.

GRAPE PICKING

Harvest time was very busy. These men are picking grapes and carrying them in buckets to the press. The squeezed juice was turned into wine.

TRAMPLED UNDER FOOT

These bound Libyans, painted on the soles of shoes, symbolized Egypt's power over foreigners. Slaves could be bought and sold like cattle, but they could also rent land and earn their freedom.

SERVANT GIRL

Most domestic servants were just poor. But some were female slaves who had escaped debt by selling themselves into slavery. The purchaser agreed to protect and feed the slave – and might later free her.

WOODEN MODEL OF SERVANT GRINDING CORN

Quern (grind stone)

MODEL WORKER

Egyptians believed that, in heaven, they would work for the gods in the *Field of Reeds*. The rich were buried with model *shabti* figures, to do the hard work for them.

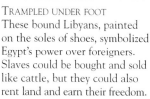

MIDDLE CLASSES

EGYPT'S EFFICIENT administration
was run by an educated middle
class of scribes and officials. Military
officers ran the army, while priests
organized prayers and offerings in the
temples. Lower on the social pyramid
were craftsworkers and traders – but
they still had a much better standard
of living than the peasant farmers.

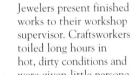

MEDICAL DOCTOR
This is one of just two known images
of a doctor at work. Many priests and
scribes were also doctors. Some
specialized in treating the eyes, teeth,
or the head. One priest had the title
"Doctor to the King's Belly."

ARTISANS
Jewelers present finished
works to their workshop
supervisor. Craftsworkers
toiled long hours in
hot, dirty conditions and
were given little personal
credit for the beautiful
works of art they produced.

A variety
of trees

Sistrum
(ceremonial rattle)

Incense
cone

The garden pool
would have
been stocked
with fish

PRIEST
In countless temples throughout the land, teams of priests and priestesses made offerings to the gods in the name of their pharaoh. In return, they were rewarded with land and a generous income.

Shrine of god Atum

SERVANT
Well-off middle-class families had servants to cook, clean, and help them wash and dress. This servant is placing an incense cone on his master's head, ready for a night out.

This official carries a wooden staff, which was a symbol of authority

SCRIBE
In most towns and villages, the only people who could read and write were scribes, which made them powerful and influential people. Art often shows them sitting cross-legged. This scribe is Pes-shu-per, c.700 B.C.

Papyrus

Vents to catch cool breeze

WELL-TO-DO COUPLE
This detail from a papyrus shows the scribe Nakhte and his wife in the garden of their villa. A platform protects the house from high floodwaters. The couple is wearing elaborately pleated clothes and heavy wigs.

OFFICIAL
The government was run by state officials, ranging from the *Vizier*, the top statesman, to local officials who ran the day-to-day affairs in each district, or *nome*.

31

THE ARMY

EGYPT'S FIGHTING forces evolved
from the Old Kingdom tradition
of mustering troops when an
emergency arose to the large,
well-equipped army of the New
Kingdom. In supreme control
was the pharaoh. Below him,
ranking officers commanded
corps of soldiers, who
fought on foot or in
chariots.

WAR GALLEY
Armed with axes and bows, the
navy fought sea battles from ships.
These had figureheads of gods and
names like "Wild Bull," "Star of
Egypt," or "Soul of the Gods."

STING OF BATTLE
The pharaoh
thanked soldiers for
bravery in battle by
giving them gold flies,
made in the royal
workshops by the
best jewelers.
Worn around
the neck, the
fly meant that
a soldier had
"stung" the enemy.

BATTLE FORMATION
In the periods of disorder that followed the Old
Kingdom's collapse, many regional princes owned
armies. This model, c.2000 B.C., from the tomb of
Prince Mesehti may represent his private army.

STANDARD TACTICS
The pharaoh and his council of war
decided on strategy. Every unit of the
Egyptian army carried a standard so that
they were easy to identify on the battle
field. Orders were given by war trumpet.

PEACE WORK

In peacetime, the army was put to work digging ditches, mining, or hauling stone for temples and pyramids. The navy went on trading expeditions. This wall carving from Queen Hatshepsut's temple shows a trip, *c*.1496 B.C., to the Land of Punt. The fleet returned with baboons and incense trees.

Domed houses on stilts

Many different trees and plants

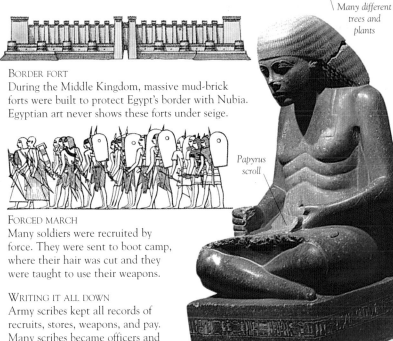

BORDER FORT

During the Middle Kingdom, massive mud-brick forts were built to protect Egypt's border with Nubia. Egyptian art never shows these forts under seige.

Papyrus scroll

FORCED MARCH

Many soldiers were recruited by force. They were sent to boot camp, where their hair was cut and they were taught to use their weapons.

WRITING IT ALL DOWN

Army scribes kept all records of recruits, stores, weapons, and pay. Many scribes became officers and went on to join the general staff, where battle tactics were decided.

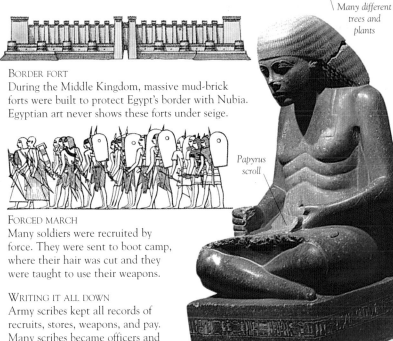

EGYPTIAN WOMEN

WOMEN HAD CLEARLY DEFINED roles. They were responsible for looking after the house and bringing up the children. Many did a lot of back-breaking labor, such as working in the fields. But, by law, women had the same rights as men. A wife could even take her husband to court if he treated her badly.

A DELAYED BEATING
Egyptian criminals were beaten. But an exception was made with pregnant women, so as not to hurt the innocent unborn child. Punishment had to wait until after the birth.

Coffins fit inside each other

BRINGING UP BABY
A woman's main job was raising children. Mothers carried babies in slings. If a wife did not bear a son, her husband would take a mistress, and the family would adopt the child.

GOLDEN PRIESTESS
"Priestess" was one of the few titles women could have. Another was "Player of Music in the Temple." These golden coffins belong to Henutmehit, a priestess of the city of Thebes, c.1250 B.C.

MARRIED COUPLE
This happy-looking couple is Katep and his wife Hetepheres, c.2500 B.C. Some unions were arranged, but other Egyptians married for love. Men could have several wives, but the marriage contract protected the wife and children, so most men could only afford one.

Woman's pale skin suggests she stayed in the home

BREAST MILK JUG
Mothers breastfed their babies openly. One carving even shows Queen Nefertiti nursing her daughter. Excess milk may have been kept in jugs like this. Mothers with a short supply prayed to the goddess Isis.

Woman carries basket on head

NEFERTITI
This statue of the beloved wife of king Akhenaten was found in a sculptor's workshop in Amarna. After her husband's death, Nefertiti may even have ruled on her own under a false name.

A WOMAN KING
Hatshepsut was the first woman to become a true pharaoh (1479–1457 B.C.). Like other pharaohs, Hatshepsut had herself portrayed as a sphinx.

Ceremonial beard

Face of Hatshepsut

Base fitted in stand

WOMAN'S WORK
Many women were household servants. Others worked as wet nurses, bakers, weavers, singers, dancers, musicians, and even doctors. But women never held public office.

THE PHARAOH

EGYPTIANS BELIEVED their pharaoh was a living god. He alone could unite the country and maintain the cosmic order, or *Ma'at*. They believed that, when he died, he would achieve eternal life – not just for himself, but also for his people. The pharaoh's power was absolute. He led the army, set taxes, judged criminals, and controlled the temples.

HORUS
The pharaoh was associated with the gods of the sun and sky, especially the falcon-headed sky god Horus.

Thutmose IV

ROYAL NAME
A pharaoh's name was written inside a cartouche. This oval loop symbolized the king's power over "all that the sun encircles."

KING OF THE NILE
Hapy was the god of the Nile flood. He was portrayed as a king, wearing the royal *nemes* headdress and false beard. The woman's breasts were symbolic of his waters, which gave life to Egypt.

ANKH
The ankh was the symbol of life. In art, only gods or kings carry this symbol. Many paintings show a god or goddess giving life to a pharaoh by touching his mouth with the ankh.

SYMBOLS OF THE PHARAOH
Tutankhamun carries a crook and flail and wears the striped *nemes* headcloth and ceremonial beard. The vulture and cobra on his brow represent Upper and Lower Egypt, respectively.

The Uraeus
(*said to spit fire at the king's enemies*)

Vulture goddess Nekhbet

Nemes headcloth

PEPY II
This pharaoh ruled for 94 years. Every 30 years the pharaoh was recrowned in the *Sed* festival, a jubilee celebration. The highlight was a race in which the king ran a course to prove his fitness to rule.

False beard

Crook

OSTRICH-FEATHER FAN
The pharaoh was almighty. Servants fanned him, and visitors kissed the ground before him. But anyone touching him without permission could be sentenced to death.

37

THE ROYAL HOUSE

IMPORTANT OFFICIALS were called "Friends of the Pharaoh." They had titles like "Fanbearer on the Right of the King" and "Master of the Horse." Many of them lived at the palace. On great state occasions, they would be joined by high priests and officials from all over Egypt.

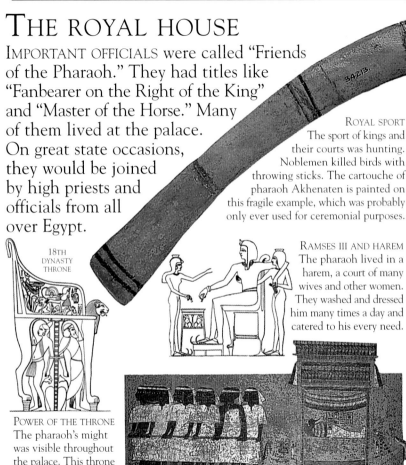

ROYAL SPORT
The sport of kings and their courts was hunting. Noblemen killed birds with throwing sticks. The cartouche of pharaoh Akhenaten is painted on this fragile example, which was probably only ever used for ceremonial purposes.

18TH DYNASTY THRONE

RAMSES III AND HAREM
The pharaoh lived in a harem, a court of many wives and other women. They washed and dressed him many times a day and catered to his every need.

POWER OF THE THRONE
The pharaoh's might was visible throughout the palace. This throne has bound captives under the seat, showing the king's control over foreigners and his role as defender of Egypt.

TUTANKHAMUN'S OFFICIALS
A painting in Tutankhamun's tomb shows the court officials dragging the king's coffin at his funeral. In his lifetime, they would have helped the king in the day-to-day affairs of state.

PREGNANT QUEEN

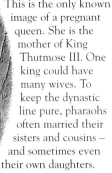

This is the only known image of a pregnant queen. She is the mother of King Thutmose III. One king could have many wives. To keep the dynastic line pure, pharaohs often married their sisters and cousins – and sometimes even their own daughters.

A PRINCE

It was very important for the pharaoh to have an heir. If his chief wife had no sons, a boy born by one of his other wives became heir. If he had no sons, the next pharaoh could start a new dynasty.

RAMESSIDE
QUEEN

COURT OFFICIAL

This is Sennefer and his wife. He was "Prince of the Southern City" (Thebes) and "Administrator of Granaries" in *c.*1400 B.C. Sennefer's wife was a royal wet nurse.

GODDESS QUEEN

The pharaoh's chief wife ruled beside him as his queen. She was also looked upon as a god on earth. The king represented the all-powerful sun god, while she was associated with Hathor, goddess of love, and Isis, the mother goddess.

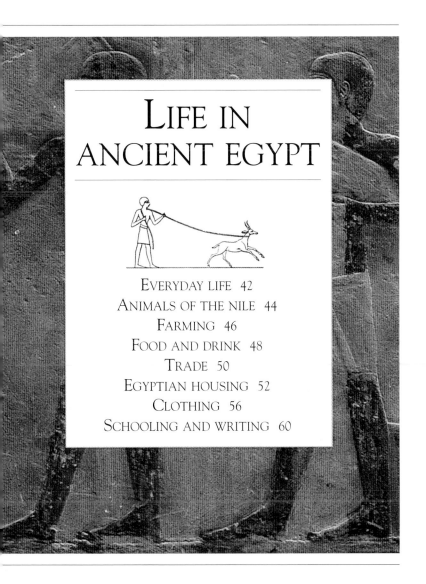

LIFE IN ANCIENT EGYPT

EVERYDAY LIFE

EGYPTIAN LIFE revolved around three seasons. During the flood, *akhet* (July to October), farm work stopped. *Peret*, the time of plowing and sowing, began when the waters went down in November. The busiest season was *shemu*, the harvest. From March to June, farmers worked hard to bring in the crops before the river rose again.

IRRIGATION DEVICE
Farmers used *shadufs* to raise water from the river. They irrigated the land by using a system of canals and dikes.

PYRAMID
Thousands of farmers had nothing to do during the flood season. So they joined the pharaoh's skilled labor force to work on huge building projects like temples or pyramids. This is the remains of the Meidum pyramid, built around 2550 B.C. for the pharaoh Sneferu.

Limestone core of pyramid

Farmland on edge of desert

HUNTING IN THE MARSHES
Work and play centered on the Nile. This tomb carving shows cattle being herded across the river. The calf being helped into a boat is about to be grabbed by a crocodile.

In the Old Kingdom, silver was far rarer than gold

THE SIDELOCK OF YOUTH
Children often ran around naked in the hot climate. They are usually shown with a distinctive hairstyle.

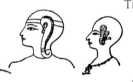

RINGS
Both men and women enjoyed wearing jewelry, which was often made from precious metals. These swivel-top rings have scarab beetles and good-luck designs engraved on them.

CATTLE COUNT
This wooden model shows the cattle count, an event that took place every year or so. This was a means of assessing a person's wealth. The cattle are driven past scribes, who write down the numbers for the owner's tax records.

43

ANIMALS OF THE NILE

IN ANCIENT TIMES, a great variety of animals thrived in Egypt. The desert was home to lions, wolves, antelopes, wild bulls, and hares. The river marshes echoed with the loud cries of exotic birds. Crocodiles lazed on the banks, while hippos wallowed in the water. At night, owls, jackals, and hyenas came out in search of food.

CAT MUMMY
Sacred to the goddess Bastet, cats were popular pets. Cats were often mummified and buried in cat-shaped coffins after they died.

CROCODILE GOD
Many people were killed by the huge Nile crocodiles. The animal was worshipped as the god Sobek.

ANIMAL GAMES
This comical papyrus gives us a glimpse of ancient Egyptian humor. Like the lion and antelope playing senet, the animals are all doing things that are wildly out of character.

Senet was a popular board game

Mouth poured perfume

Ripples for scales

FLASK
Fish such as perch and catfish were caught up and down the river. This fish-shaped glass flask poured perfume from its mouth.

WILD SHEEP
This figurine may once have graced the dressing table of a wealthy lady. It is a cosmetic container in the shape of a wild sheep, an animal that still roams the fringes of the Sahara today.

Lid of container

Crouching cat

Water-plant design

HIPPO
This animal was feared because it overturned boats. In legend, it was associated with the evil god Seth, so killing a hippo was a symbolic victory over evil. The wealthy hunted them with spears.

Jackals herd goats

A cat tends a flock of geese

Lion and ox play

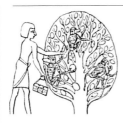

PICKING FIGS
Ancient Egyptians
loved sycamore figs.
So did baboons,
which were trained
to climb the trees
and pick the fruit.

FARMING

EGYPTIAN LIFE was based on farming the rich flood plain of the Nile. The main crops were emmer wheat, barley, and flax. Farmers also grew beans, lentils, onions, leeks, cucumbers, and lettuce in garden plots, and fruits like grapes, dates, figs, and pomegranates. Animals raised for meat included cattle, pigs, sheep, goats, geese, and ducks.

Scribes making
tax records

Wooden chest

Tomb owner

Man with jars
of water

Man drinking
water from jar

Mother with
baby

Workers cutting
grain with sickles

Men carrying
grain in basket

PLOUGHING THE FIELDS

This wooden tomb model shows a man plowing. The wooden plow is being pulled by two oxen. The plowman used a hoe if he needed to break up any heavy clumps of soil. Another man would have followed behind, sowing seed.

Man guides plow

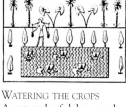

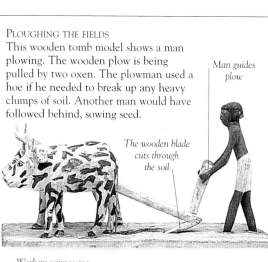

The wooden blade cuts through the soil

WATERING THE CROPS

A network of dykes, pools, and irrigation channels crisscrossed the farmland. Here, a man is carrying buckets of water hung on a yoke across his shoulders.

Workers winnowing

HARVESTING GRAIN

This is a harvesting scene from a tomb. Below, workers cut the grain and load it into baskets. Above, other workers are winnowing – throwing the grain into the air to separate it from the chaff. Scribes record the quantity.

Protective headcloth

LENTILS

Girls squabbling about leftover wheat *Linen kilt*

DATES

WHEAT

CROPS

The fertile soil by the Nile enabled Egyptian farmers to grow a large variety of crops. Harvested grain was stored in granaries and used to make bread and beer.

FOOD AND DRINK

BREAD AND BEER were the two staples in an Egyptian's diet. Both were made in a similar way, using wheat or barley. Bakers also made a whole variety of cakes and pastries, often sweetened with dates or honey. There were many fruits and vegetables, but potatoes and citrus fruits were unknown. The wealthy enjoyed lavish banquets – feasting on meat, washed down with wine. Poor people were more likely to dine on fish and beer.

HONEY
Egyptians were the first people known to keep bees. Honey was collected to sweeten cakes, beer, and wine.

Wooden siphon

BEER STRAINER

Holes for straining

GRAPES

GRAPES AND WINE
Wall-paintings show workers picking grapes and squeezing them in a press. The wine matured in tall amphorae, inscribed with the year, type of grape, region, and vineyard owner.

WINEPRESS

BREWING BEER
Women made beer. They mixed bread dough with yeast and left it to ferment in large vats. A few weeks later, they filtered the mash. The mature beer was seasoned with spices or dates. It was very thick and had to be strained before drinking.

FOOD OFFERINGS

Egyptians brought food to temples and tombs to make sure the gods and spirits of the dead were well fed. This tomb carving shows bearers bringing a selection of offerings.

EVERYDAY FARE

Fruit, vegetables, and grain were grown in plenty. The Egyptians ate bread with every meal. Until the New Kingdom, when bakeries became common, most housewives made their own bread. Loaves came in many shapes, some made specially for religious rites such as offerings for the dead. This bread was placed in a tomb more than 3,000 years ago.

Baboons could not resist figs

MODERN
FIGS

BREAD

MODERN
DATES

AT THE BUTCHERS

This tomb model shows an ox being slaughtered. The meat would be roasted, boiled, or stewed. Rich Egyptians ate a lot of meat, which was often wild game from the hunt. Antelope, gazelle, porcupine, hare, and fowl such as quail and crane were all on the menu.

ANCIENT PALM
TREE FRUIT

49

EGGS FOR THE PHARAOH
Ostrich plumes and eggs
were often among the
tributes sent to pharaohs
from lands in the south.

TRADE

FOR MOST OF ITS HISTORY, ancient
Egypt was the richest country in
the world. The Egyptians grew more
than enough food. So the surplus
grain, along with linen, papyrus,
and dried fish, was exported in
exchange for luxury

Ebony   *Red jasper*

items such as incense, silver, and
fine cedar wood. Horses came
from Asia to the east, while,
to the south, Nubia and
Punt were a source of
gold, ivory, ebony,
and incense.

Incense

Gold rings

Giraffe tails

NUBIAN GIFTS
These Nubian envoys
are taking gifts to the
Egyptian court. Nubia
was rich in copper,
gold, and semiprecious
stones. Merchants also
supplied Egypt with
exotic goods like incense
and wild animals, brought
from lands farther south.

Live baboon

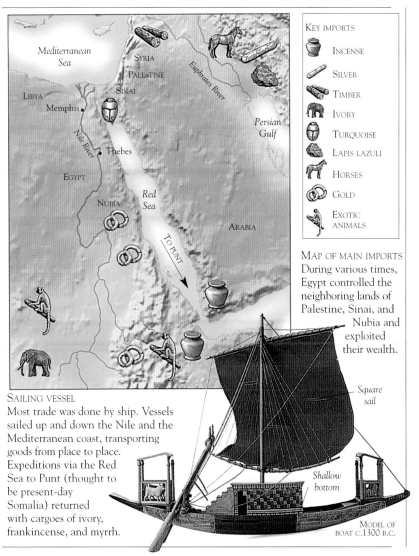

KEY IMPORTS

- INCENSE
- SILVER
- TIMBER
- IVORY
- TURQUOISE
- LAPIS LAZULI
- HORSES
- GOLD
- EXOTIC ANIMALS

Mediterranean Sea

SYRIA
PALESTINE
SINAI
Euphrates River
LIBYA
Memphis
Persian Gulf
Nile River
Thebes
EGYPT
NUBIA
Red Sea
ARABIA
TO PUNT

MAP OF MAIN IMPORTS
During various times, Egypt controlled the neighboring lands of Palestine, Sinai, and Nubia and exploited their wealth.

SAILING VESSEL
Most trade was done by ship. Vessels sailed up and down the Nile and the Mediterranean coast, transporting goods from place to place. Expeditions via the Red Sea to Punt (thought to be present-day Somalia) returned with cargoes of ivory, frankincense, and myrrh.

Square sail

Shallow bottom

MODEL OF BOAT C.1300 B.C.

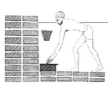

MAKING BRICKS
Wet Nile mud was mixed with sand and straw, squeezed into a wooden mold, and then dried in the sun.

EGYPTIAN HOUSING

EGYPTIAN HOMES were built to stay cool. From pharaoh's palace to worker's hut, most houses were made from mud bricks. Many dwellings had roof terraces, where people could take the air in hot weather. Wealthy families lived in large villas with lush gardens and fish-stocked pools. In the cities, the poorer people lived in simple homes, crammed together in a maze of alleys, passageways, and squares.

ANCIENT FRESCOES
The walls and ceilings of rich people's houses were painted with colorful designs, often composed of geometric patterns and plant motifs.

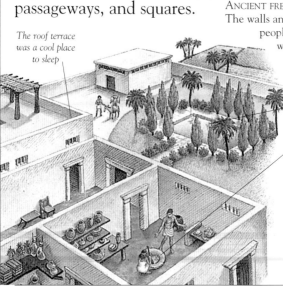

The roof terrace was a cool place to sleep

Decorative pond

Kitchen area with open fire for cooking

INSIDE A HOUSE
In a typical house of a well-off Egyptian, the main living area was placed some way from the kitchen to avoid cooking smells. Some bedrooms had their own bathing facilities and lavatories.

Flat roof

Stairs to upper story

Chair

Colonnaded entrance

Bed

Food was stored and cooked in courtyard

SIMPLE HOME

This pottery house (*c*.1900 B.C.) was placed in a tomb for the owner's use in the next life and shows architectural details that existed in houses of the period.

HOUSE FACTS

• Mud bricks were sometimes stamped with the name of the reigning pharaoh.

• A workman's week was nine days long – the tenth was a day of rest.

• Windows were small to keep out hot sunlight.

A VILLAGE ON THE NILE TODAY

Egyptian houses are still made of mud bricks. Some towns now sit on hills because they have been rebuilt again and again on the ruins of older settlements.

In the home

Egyptian houses were sparsely furnished. Tables were rare, and many pictures show people squatting cross-legged on the floor rather than sitting on stools. Most people slept on benches built into the walls; only the wealthy had real beds. The pieces of furniture that have survived have simple, elegant lines. Many are exquisitely crafted, with inlays of gemstones, glass, and precious woods.

NOBLE CHAIRS
Only a wealthy Egyptian household would have chairs. Like tables, these were usually low and wide. Legs were often carved to look like lions' paws or bulls' hooves.

SERVANT LOOKING AFTER FIRE

Fanning flames

Special base holds jar steady

JAR STAND
Lamps and jars often sat on wooden stands. Oil lamps were the only means of artificial light. Oil was expensive, so many poorer people went to bed early and rose at dawn.

Carved decoration   *Bow*

Painted legs   *Firestick*

String

FIRE
This is the only type of Egyptian fire-making device found. A stick was pushed into a wooden base, while a bow looped around the stick was moved quickly back and forth. The friction set the base on fire.

End of stick fits into groove   *Base*   *Grooves blackened by fire*

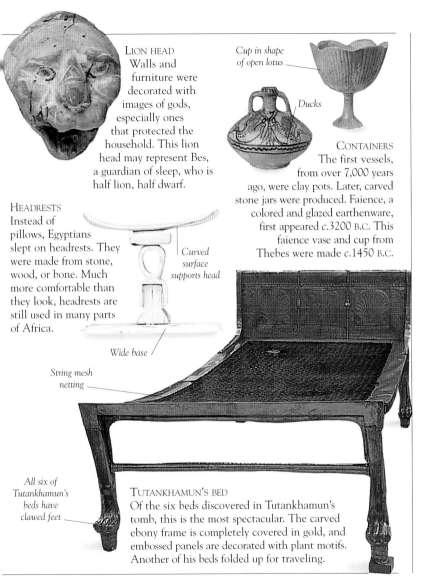

LION HEAD
Walls and furniture were decorated with images of gods, especially ones that protected the household. This lion head may represent Bes, a guardian of sleep, who is half lion, half dwarf.

Cup in shape of open lotus

Ducks

CONTAINERS
The first vessels, from over 7,000 years ago, were clay pots. Later, carved stone jars were produced. Faience, a colored and glazed earthenware, first appeared c.3200 B.C. This faience vase and cup from Thebes were made c.1450 B.C.

HEADRESTS
Instead of pillows, Egyptians slept on headrests. They were made from stone, wood, or bone. Much more comfortable than they look, headrests are still used in many parts of Africa.

Curved surface supports head

Wide base

String mesh netting

All six of Tutankhamun's beds have clawed feet

TUTANKHAMUN'S BED
Of the six beds discovered in Tutankhamun's tomb, this is the most spectacular. The carved ebony frame is completely covered in gold, and embossed panels are decorated with plant motifs. Another of his beds folded up for traveling.

CLOTHING

EGYPTIANS WORE simple linen clothes. Men dressed in short kilts, leaving their chests bare or draping a cloak or a strip of linen over their shoulders. Women wore long, tight-fitting dresses. On cool evenings they might put on a long-sleeved gown as well. In later periods, tunics and dresses with complicated pleats became popular. Both women and men wore wigs.

Damp cloth was pressed into grooves

PLEAT BOARD

PRESSED PLEATS
Grooved boards like this may have been used to pleat the clothes of well-to-do Egyptians.

COARSE LINEN
Ordinary Egyptians wore coarse linen, while the rich dressed in a lighter, finer cloth. Finest of all was the semitransparent "royal linen." The Egyptians knew about dyes, but most linen was left a natural white.

Interwoven flax fibers

OFFICIAL ATTIRE
This is Mereruka, *vizier* to King Teti in about 2340 B.C. He is wearing the short kilt typical of the Old Kingdom. The kilt was tied at the waist, often in an elaborate bow.

ROYAL DRESS

Egyptians were not prudish about their bodies. Kings are often shown in tiny kilts, and queens wore near transparent dresses. For important ceremonies, the king wore a long kilt and an elaborate cloak with countless pleats.

COURT LADY

Clothes were draped rather than cut to fit. The fringed, finely pleated dress of this noblewoman leaves one shoulder bare and reaches well below her ankles. Her heavy, braided wig is crowned with a circlet of flowers.

WEAVING LINEN

Women combed the stems of the flax plant to remove the spiky heads. Then they separated the fibers from the stalk and spun them on a spindle, weighted by a whorl. The spun threads were woven on a loom to make cloth.

Whorl

SPINDLE

FLAX COMB

Twine strap

DRESS FACTS

• Priests dressed statues of gods each morning and undressed them at night.

• Some peasants and fishermen worked naked.

• The wealthy used professional laundries. Poorer people did their washing in the river.

SANDALS

Most Egyptians went barefoot. But priests and wealthy people wore sandals. These were made from leather or reeds like papyrus that flourished in the marshes by the Nile.

Rotating spindle twists fibers

Jewelry and makeup

The Egyptians went to great lengths to look good. Men and women rubbed oil into their skins, painted their eyes with thick makeup, and sprinkled their clothes with sweet-smelling perfumes. At parties, women crowned their wigs with incense cones. These melted slowly, pouring scent onto their hair and clothes. The wealthy wore gold jewelry that sparkled with semiprecious stones.

Malachite

Galena

COLOR
Green eye paint came from malachite, black eye *kohl* from galena, and red for lips was made from iron oxide.

Iron oxide

EARRINGS

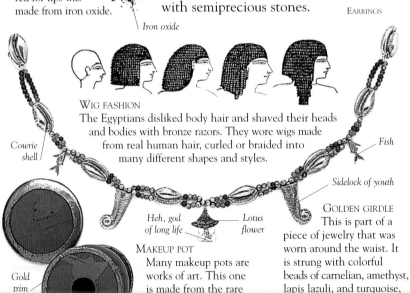

WIG FASHION
The Egyptians disliked body hair and shaved their heads and bodies with bronze razors. They wore wigs made from real human hair, curled or braided into many different shapes and styles.

Cowrie shell

Fish

Sidelock of youth

Heh, god of long life

Lotus flower

MAKEUP POT
Many makeup pots are works of art. This one is made from the rare blue stone anhydrite.

Gold trim

GOLDEN GIRDLE
This is part of a piece of jewelry that was worn around the waist. It is strung with colorful beads of carnelian, amethyst, lapis lazuli, and turquoise, plus gold good-luck charms.

COSMETIC PALETTE
This makeup container is carved and painted to look like a bunch of flowers. The buds are circles of ivory, dyed a soft pink. The swiveling top hides a hollow where cosmetic cream was stored.

BRACELET
Cobras protect the sky god Horus on this bracelet made for a prince.

Top swivels sideways

Polished metal surface

Lotus-style headdress

Handle in shape of serving girl

Duck   *Leaves*

METAL MIRROR
The Egyptians did not have glass mirrors. Instead, they admired their reflections in polished disks of copper or bronze. The bright, shining surfaces reminded the Egyptians of the sun they worshipped.

Glass container with applicator

MAKEUP FOR EYES
Kohl was kept in pots and applied with thin metal tools. Even children wore *kohl*, which also protected against eye infections.

59

SCHOOLING AND WRITING

MOST EGYPTIAN CHILDREN did not go to school. To be a goldsmith or a painter, a boy trained in a workshop or with a team of workers building a tomb. Scribes were given a more formal education, starting at age nine and lasting about five years. They had to study hard and were beaten if they were lazy. But it was worth it – scribes were among the only people who could read or write, which gave them status.

Layers placed at right angles

MAKING PAPYRUS
Paper was made from papyrus reed. The soft pith was cut into strips, placed in two layers, then pounded together to form a strong sheet.

Hieratic text always reads right to left

THREE SCRIPTS
Egyptian picture-writings are called hieroglyphs, the Greek word for "sacred carvings." Scribes later developed two other scripts, hieratic and demotic, which were much quicker to write.

Hieroglyphs read either left to right or right to left. They were written downward in columns or in horizontal lines

When figures face left, reader starts on left-hand side

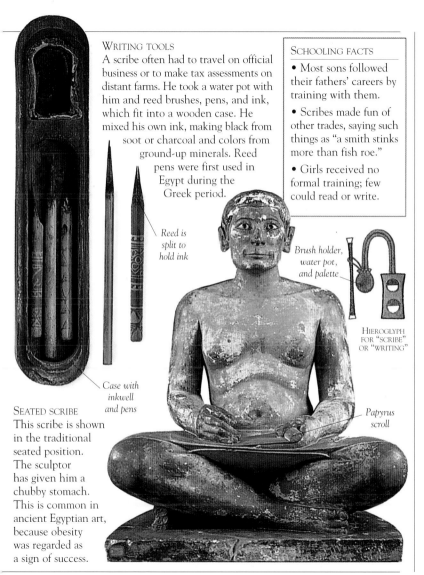

WRITING TOOLS

A scribe often had to travel on official business or to make tax assessments on distant farms. He took a water pot with him and reed brushes, pens, and ink, which fit into a wooden case. He mixed his own ink, making black from soot or charcoal and colors from ground-up minerals. Reed pens were first used in Egypt during the Greek period.

SCHOOLING FACTS

• Most sons followed their fathers' careers by training with them.

• Scribes made fun of other trades, saying such things as "a smith stinks more than fish roe."

• Girls received no formal training; few could read or write.

Reed is split to hold ink

Brush holder, water pot, and palette

HIEROGLYPH FOR "SCRIBE" OR "WRITING"

Case with inkwell and pens

SEATED SCRIBE

This scribe is shown in the traditional seated position. The sculptor has given him a chubby stomach. This is common in ancient Egyptian art, because obesity was regarded as a sign of success.

Papyrus scroll

61

Deciphering hieroglyphs

For nearly 1,500 years, no one could read hieroglyphs, the ancient Egyptian picture-writing. The French scholar Jean-François Champollion spent most of his life trying to break the code. He made his first breakthrough in 1822, while studying the Rosetta Stone, and soon experts were able to read the inscriptions that cover many Egyptian artifacts.

The text is a message of thanks to Pharaoh Ptolemy V

Demotic

The loop represents eternity

ROYAL NAMES

A pharaoh's name was written inside an oval loop called a cartouche. This piece of jewelry contains the cartouche of Senusret II.

Sa	Ankh	N	Ra	Nefer
Son	Life	Water	Day	Beautiful

PICTURES FOR WORDS AND SOUNDS

One hieroglyph can stand for either a word or a sound. For instance, a scribe would draw a goose both for the sound "sa" and the word "son."

A name of a pharaoh can be recognized because it is written within a cartouche

Hieroglyphs

JEAN-FRANÇOIS CHAMPOLLION (1790–1832)
A brilliant linguist, Champollion had mastered 12 languages by age 16. The first hieroglyphs he deciphered were pharaohs' names. By 1824, he had translated most of the symbols and begun to unravel Egyptian grammar.

"PTOLEMY" IN HIEROGLYPHS

"PTOLEMY" IN DEMOTIC

ΠΤΟΛΕΜΑΙΟΣ

"PTOLEMY" IN GREEK

THE ROSETTA STONE
Inscribed in 196 B.C., the Rosetta Stone was unearthed again in 1799. The text is repeated in hieroglyphs, demotic, and Greek. Champollion could read Greek, and so he used this text to translate the other two scripts.

CRACKING THE CODE
The English physicist Thomas Young was the first to recognize the hieroglyphs for Ptolemy and Cleopatra on the Rosetta Stone. But Champollion made the great breakthrough when he realized that some symbols stood for ideas while others were simply sounds.

P   T   O   L   M   Y   S

K   L   E   O   P   A   T   R   A

Greek

The Stone is a slab of black basalt, found near Rosetta in the delta

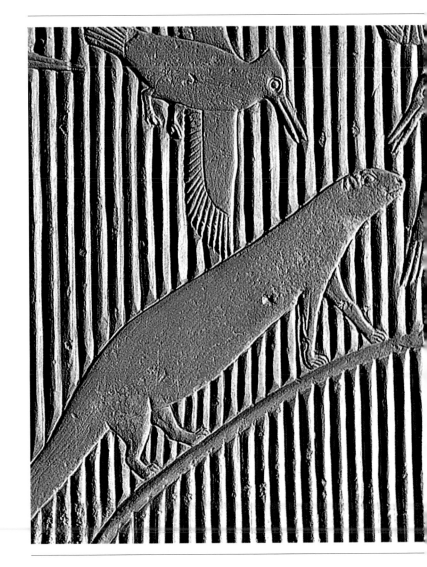

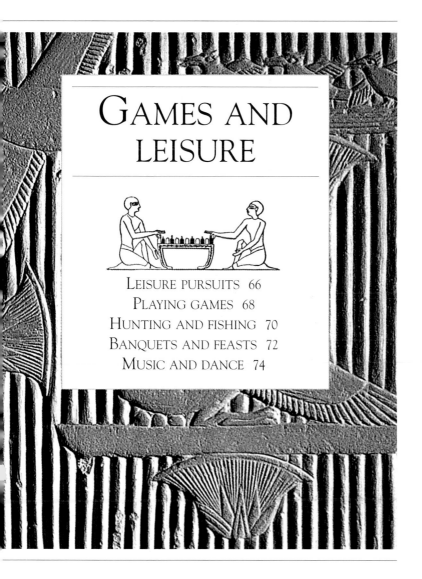

GAMES AND LEISURE

LEISURE PURSUITS

THE EGYPTIANS LIVED LIFE to the full. At public festivals and private parties, they feasted and drank, entertained by singers, dancers, and musicians. Children played out in the sunshine, while adults reveled in sports like hunting and fishing. In quieter moments they wrote poetry or enjoyed board games.

ANGLING
Egyptians were the first people to fish for pure pleasure. Nobles are often shown in armchairs, lazily dangling lines into their well-stocked garden pools.

ENTERTAINERS AT A BANQUET
Party scenes show how much the Egyptians liked music and dance. In this tomb painting, c.1400 B.C., one woman plays a double flute while others clap along or dance to the beat. In Egyptian art, it is very unusual to see faces front on.

LEISURE FACTS

• Egyptians swam backstroke and crawl. Upper-class children were given lessons.

• Farmworkers and fishermen had their own working songs.

• Festival revelers sailing on Nile barges sometimes "mooned" the crowd on the shore.

STONE THROWER
This is the earliest known example of a sling. It dates from about 1900 B.C. and was found in the town of Kahun in the Faiyum Oasis. The sling was probably used to scare birds away from Kahun's vineyards and lush gardens. One end of the cord was looped around a finger to keep hold of the sling after firing.

Woven cord

Loop for finger

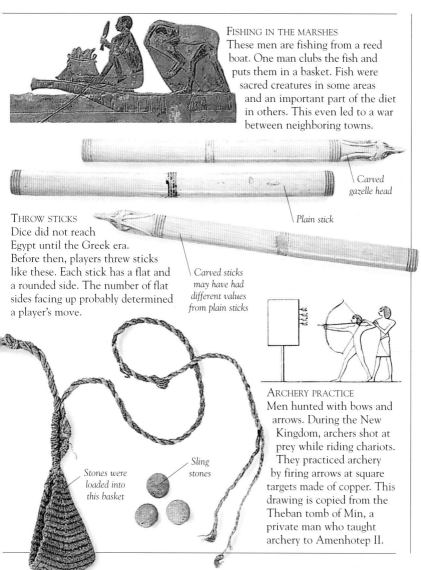

FISHING IN THE MARSHES

These men are fishing from a reed boat. One man clubs the fish and puts them in a basket. Fish were sacred creatures in some areas and an important part of the diet in others. This even led to a war between neighboring towns.

Carved gazelle head

Plain stick

THROW STICKS

Dice did not reach Egypt until the Greek era. Before then, players threw sticks like these. Each stick has a flat and a rounded side. The number of flat sides facing up probably determined a player's move.

Carved sticks may have had different values from plain sticks

ARCHERY PRACTICE

Men hunted with bows and arrows. During the New Kingdom, archers shot at prey while riding chariots. They practiced archery by firing arrows at square targets made of copper. This drawing is copied from the Theban tomb of Min, a private man who taught archery to Amenhotep II.

Stones were loaded into this basket

Sling stones

67

PLAYING GAMES

IN THE WARM EGYPTIAN CLIMATE, boys and girls spent a lot of time outdoors, swimming, dancing, riding donkeys, and enjoying games of leapfrog and tug-of-war. They played with balls, dolls, toy animals, and pets such as cats, birds, and monkeys. The most popular board game for adults was called senet. Tutankhamun liked it so much that he was buried with four complete boards.

TOPS
Children spun these pottery tops with a twist of the fingers or a quick tug on a piece of string wrapped round the toy.

CLAY BALLS
Balls made of papyrus, cloth, and leather have all been found. These brightly painted clay balls were once filled with seeds or tiny lumps of clay to make them rattle when thrown.

String to move lower jaw

CAT TOY
Pulling the string on this carved wooden cat makes it open and close its mouth. Other ancient animal toys have glass eyes, movable legs and arms, and tails that wag.

CATCHING AND JUGGLING
This scene is copied from a Middle Kingdom tomb. These jugglers may have been professionals or people playing for fun or ritual.

HORSES AND MUMMIES

This wooden horse could be pulled along with a string through its nose. Nile mud animals, birds, and even tiny mummies lying in their coffins have been found. These may be toys made by children or votive offerings.

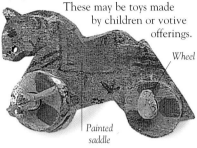

Wheel

Painted saddle

Senet

A GAME OF SENET

Senet was played by moving counters on a board of 30 squares – some were dangerous to land on, others were lucky. Unfortunately, the rules have been lost.

Fighting with wooden sticks

TOURNAMENTS

Men competed in games of boxing, wrestling, and fencing. King Ramses III held the first recorded fencing tournament in c.1250 B.C. Egyptian and allied soldiers fought with wooden sticks.

Winning position

Hieroglyph of pharaoh's name

SNAKE GAME

This was one of the earliest Egyptian board games. The playing surface is the shape of a coiled snake. Players started at the tip of the tail and tried to move balls toward the snake's head at the center.

HUNTING AND FISHING

THE MAIN SPORT for well-to-do Egyptians was hunting. In early times, nobles stalked antelope, bulls, and lions on foot; later they hunted from horse-drawn chariots. Pharaohs were proud of their kills. Amenhotep III boasted of 102 lions in ten years as king, and Thutmose III claimed 120 elephants during one trip to Syria.

MAN WITH ANTELOPE
A man returns from the hunt. Trained dogs or even hyenas were used to catch antelope or to chase them into traps.

HUNTING WITH NETS
Marsh hunters netted both fish and wildfowl. They snared birds by baiting nets with corn or maggots.

FISHING FROM RAFTS
Egyptians fished for food and fun. During the Old Kingdom, fish were usually netted or speared. Later, angling became popular. The fishermen in this tomb relief are using hooks and nets to catch the fish.

Papyrus
thicket

Throwing
stick

Wife

Duck
decoy

Daughter
steadies raft

HUNTING HYENAS

Hyenas got into game reserves and were killed along with animals kept there as quarry. They were also hunted as a menace to domestic flocks.

FOWLING

Nobles preferred to hunt birds with a throwing stick. It was like a boomerang and killed a bird by breaking its neck. This man has brought his family, including pet cat, on the hunt.

HIPPO HUNTING

These three men are spearing hippos from a papyrus raft. Spearheads were attached to long pieces of rope, so that the dying hippo could be hauled onto land.

LUTIST
Hosts hired
musicians to
play and sing
at the feast.

BANQUETS AND FEASTS

EGYPTIANS HELD FEASTS to celebrate births,
marriages, and religious festivals, or just to
entertain friends. The wealthy enjoyed
holding dinner parties. Cooks prepared a
huge meal, flavored with imported herbs
and spices. Dressed in their best clothes,
guests sat on chairs or
cushions on the floor, eating
food with their fingers
and drinking large
quantities of wine.

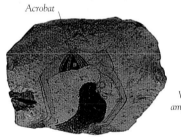

Acrobat

Wine
amphorae

AFTER-DINNER ENTERTAINMENT
Dinner parties were one of the main
sources of employment for dancers,
acrobats, and other entertainers. They
performed after the meal was finished.

NEW KINGDOM BANQUET
This scene shows Egyptian hospitality
at a dinner party. An army of servants
ply the guests with food, wine, and presents.

Food is piled
high on tables

TOO DRUNK TO WALK
Guests sometimes drank too much; some even vomited into bowls. These drunk men are being carried home from a party.

FOOD FOR THE FEAST
Pictures showing food offerings give us a good idea of the types of foods that wealthy hosts could serve their guests.

Scantily clad serving girl

Pleated clothes

Necklace presented as gift

Married couples sit arm in arm

Chair legs shaped like lions' paws

Incense cones

Servants offer wine and lotus flowers to guests

This group of women sitting together are probably unmarried

73

MUSIC AND DANCE

NO EGYPTIAN CELEBRATION would have been complete without music and dancing. At parties, singers performed to the music of harps, lutes, drums, flutes, and tambourines. Festival crowds chanted and clapped, carried along by the vibrant rhythm of Egyptian orchestras, while dancers leapt and twirled. Work, too, was often accompanied by music.

WOMAN PLAYING THE HARP
This model of a harpist was placed in a tomb to entertain guests at parties in the afterlife. In tomb pictures, harpists are often blind men.

SINGING ALONG
Singing played an important role in Egyptian music. These young women sing and dance, while beating tambourines and handheld drums.

Double crown of Egypt

CYMBALS
We do not know how Egyptian music sounded because it was never written down. The people played a wide range of instruments, suggesting that their music was varied. These bronze cymbals were used for rhythm and beat.

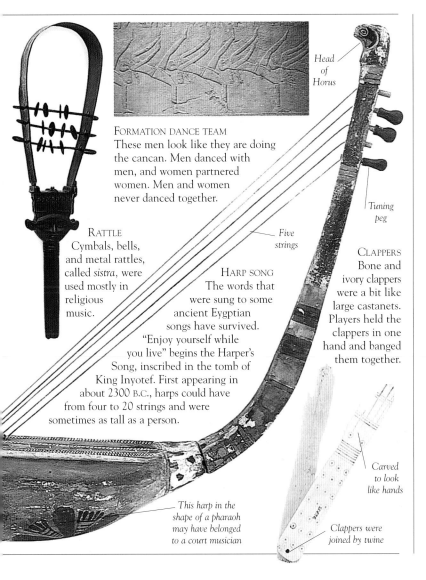

Head of Horus

FORMATION DANCE TEAM
These men look like they are doing the cancan. Men danced with men, and women partnered women. Men and women never danced together.

Tuning peg

RATTLE
Cymbals, bells, and metal rattles, called *sistra*, were used mostly in religious music.

Five strings

HARP SONG
The words that were sung to some ancient Eygptian songs have survived. "Enjoy yourself while you live" begins the Harper's Song, inscribed in the tomb of King Inyotef. First appearing in about 2300 B.C., harps could have from four to 20 strings and were sometimes as tall as a person.

CLAPPERS
Bone and ivory clappers were a bit like large castanets. Players held the clappers in one hand and banged them together.

This harp in the shape of a pharaoh may have belonged to a court musician

Carved to look like hands

Clappers were joined by twine

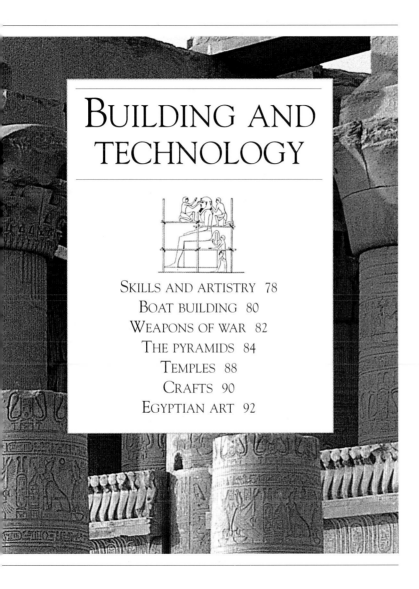

BUILDING AND TECHNOLOGY

SKILLS AND ARTISTRY

THE ANCIENT EGYPTIANS were very practical people. The great pyramids, tombs, and temples that still stand today show how they had mastered many architectural and engineering problems. These monuments were built and decorated by teams of skilled craftsmen, who worked year round for the pharaoh.

PLUMB LINE
Tools like this were used to make sure lines were vertical and to create grids for painting and carving on walls.

MUD BRICK

USING A MOLD
Wooden tomb models show scenes of ancient Egyptians at work. This man is busy molding a mud brick.

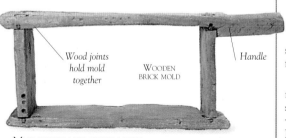

Wood joints hold mold together

WOODEN BRICK MOLD

Handle

MUD BRICK AND BRICK MOLD
The Egyptians built most of their buildings with bricks. Workmen used molds like this to shape a mixture of Nile mud, sand, and straw. Bricks were not fired, just left to dry in the hot sun.

TECHNOLOGY FACTS

• Pharaoh Khafra had 23 life-size statues of himself made for just one temple.

• The first strike in recorded history was staged by craftsmen working in the tomb of Ramses III in 1150 B.C.

• The new capital at Amarna was the first planned city in history.

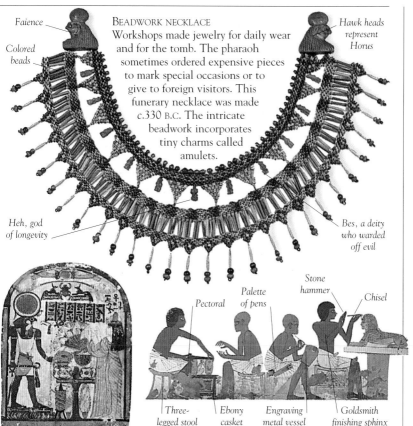

Faience

Colored beads

Hawk heads represent Horus

BEADWORK NECKLACE
Workshops made jewelry for daily wear and for the tomb. The pharaoh sometimes ordered expensive pieces to mark special occasions or to give to foreign visitors. This funerary necklace was made c.330 B.C. The intricate beadwork incorporates tiny charms called amulets.

Heh, god of longevity

Bes, a deity who warded off evil

Stone hammer

Palette of pens

Pectoral

Chisel

Three-legged stool

Ebony casket

Engraving metal vessel

Goldsmith finishing sphinx

TOMB ART
Some of the greatest art was made for the tombs of kings and nobles. On this wooden funerary stela, a priestess raises her hands in adoration of Ra-Horakhty, the falcon-headed sun god.

METALWORK
There are many paintings of craft workshops. In this detail, two jewelers finish a pectoral (pendant) and place it in a casket. To the right, a man engraves an inscription, while another is working on a golden sphinx. Other scenes in the same tomb show controllers weighing gold and checking finished articles. In reality, this workshop must have been noisy, dirty, and very hot.

79

BOAT BUILDING

EGYPT'S HIGHWAY was the Nile. Everything from grain and cattle to coffins and building stone was transported by water. Only the best boats were wooden, because wood was very rare. Most travelers and fishermen punted through the shallows on rafts made from bundles of reeds.

ADZE
Blade

STEERING OAR
The Egyptians steered their boats with special oars mounted on the stern (back). This brightly painted example was found in a boat pit near the pyramid of the pharaoh Senusret III (c.1850 B.C.). The Eye of Horus was a symbol of protection.

String

Bow

BOW DRILL

Drill bit

WOODWORKING TOOLS
A carpenter's tools have changed little since ancient Egyptian times. Saws, chisels, and axes have all been found. This adze was used for hacking and planing, while the bow drill bored holes for pegging pieces of wood together.

Man uses adze to smooth hull

CARPENTERS AT WORK
Boat building is an ancient craft. This tomb scene from Saqqara dates from about 2300 B.C. The Egyptians had not yet discovered iron, and all tools and pegs were made of copper and wood.

Sun canopy

Attendant

Mummy

Oars

MODEL BOAT
Egyptians put model
boats in tombs in the
belief that the boat
would carry the dead
person's mummy
to the afterlife.

Prow carved
to look like
a bundle
of papyrus

Five pairs
of oars

Priest

Steersman

Royal cabin

Stern

Steering
oars

KHUFU'S BOAT
The best preserved
boat is the funeral
barge of King Khufu.
It was found in 1954
in a sealed pit next
to his tomb, the Great
Pyramid at Giza. Made
from 651 pieces of
cedar, the boat is
143 ft (43.5 m) long.

NILE SAILBOAT

SEAGOING SHIP

SAILING
Large sails were used to travel
upriver against the current.
Going downriver, the sail was
dropped and the boat was rowed.

CARGO BOAT

WEAPONS OF WAR

THE ARMIES of the Old and Middle Kingdoms were small, and citizens were often called up to fight. In the New Kingdom, a more professional, permanent army was established, with corps of infantry, scouts, and marines. Chariots held two soldiers; one handled the horses and the other fired arrows at the enemy.

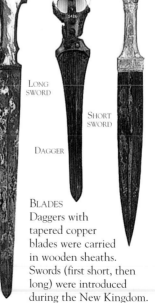

LONG
SWORD

SHORT
SWORD

DAGGER

GODDESS OF WAR
War goddess Sekhmet has a lion's head and a woman's body. She was said to stand by the pharaoh in battle, armed with arrows "with which she pierces hearts."

BLADES
Daggers with tapered copper blades were carried in wooden sheaths. Swords (first short, then long) were introduced during the New Kingdom.

FIGHTING FORMATION
Foot soldiers trained to fight in strict formation, moving together and presenting the enemy with a wall of shields. These soldiers wear kilts and carry spears.

ARROWHEADS

For thousands of years, arrowheads were made from stone (especially flint), bone, or the hardwood ebony. Bronze was not used until c.1800 B.C.

FLINT HEADS

BRONZE HEADS

CHARIOTS

Introduced from the Middle East in c.1650 B.C., chariots revolutionized warfare. Here, Tutankhamun fires arrows at Nubian enemies from the raised platform of his chariot.

ARCHER

Massed units of archers led the assault. On foot or riding in chariots, they showered the enemy with arrows. Many archers came from Nubia, which Egyptians called "the Land of the Bow."

SILVER-SHAFTED AXE

CEREMONIAL AXE

AXES

Battle-axes were used all across the Middle East. The ceremonial axe was probably awarded to a warrior for bravery.

ARCHER'S AID

An archer wore this guard on the wrist of his bow hand to protect himself from the lash of the bowstring.

SOLDIER ON HORSE

The army relied on charioteers rather than on a cavalry. This rare picture is from the Greek era.

MERCENARIES

The Egyptians supplemented their own forces by relying on foreign mercenaries, who were allowed to retain their own weapons and costumes.

BATTLE-AXE

83

GIZA

▲ TRUE PYRAMID
▲ BENT PYRAMID
▲ STEP PYRAMID

THE PYRAMIDS

ALREADY ANCIENT by Tutankhamun's times, the Pyramids of Giza have awed people ever since they were built – more than 4,500 years ago. Pyramids are tombs made to house the mummies of kings. Their massive size and the precision of their construction are amazing.

ALL THE PYRAMIDS
The biggest and best-preserved pyramids are the three at Giza. There are more than 80 others in Egypt – mostly ruins, all but buried by shifting desert sands. The first pyramids had stepped or bent sides. Then came the classic (true) shape.

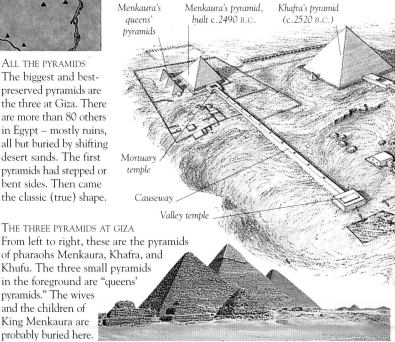

Menkaura's queens' pyramids

Menkaura's pyramid, built c.2490 B.C.

Khafra's pyramid (c.2520 B.C.)

Mortuary temple

Causeway

Valley temple

THE THREE PYRAMIDS AT GIZA
From left to right, these are the pyramids of pharaohs Menkaura, Khafra, and Khufu. The three small pyramids in the foreground are "queens' pyramids." The wives and the children of King Menkaura are probably buried here.

THE SPHINX
This massive stone figure of a lion with the head of a king crouches before the pyramid complex at Giza. The Sphinx's face is believed to be a likeness of pharaoh Khafra.

PYRAMID FACTS
• The Pyramids of Giza are one of the seven wonders of the ancient world and the only one still standing.

• The four sides of the Great Pyramid are aligned exactly with true north, south, east, and west.

• A dream told Thutmose IV to free the Sphinx from the sands that buried it.

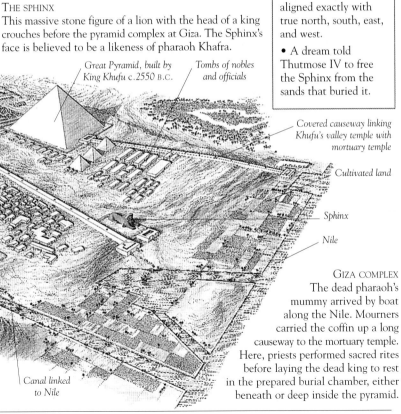

Great Pyramid, built by King Khufu c.2550 B.C.

Tombs of nobles and officials

Covered causeway linking Khufu's valley temple with mortuary temple

Cultivated land

Sphinx

Nile

Canal linked to Nile

GIZA COMPLEX
The dead pharaoh's mummy arrived by boat along the Nile. Mourners carried the coffin up a long causeway to the mortuary temple. Here, priests performed sacred rites before laying the dead king to rest in the prepared burial chamber, either beneath or deep inside the pyramid.

85

How were pyramids built?

Egyptologists estimate that it took 100,000 men 20 years to build the Great Pyramid at Giza. But how was it built? The most popular theory is that workers slid the massive blocks of stone up ramps onto the pyramid. As little real evidence exists, we will probably never know for sure.

SQUARING OFF
One tomb painting shows masons using chisels and mallets to smooth down blocks of stone.

RAMPS OR LIFTING MACHINES?
An ancient Greek traveler wrote that workers had used lifting machines to raise stones. But he was told this 2,000 years after the pyramids were built. Ramps are less work and thus more likely.

Four times as many men

WERE THE PYRAMIDS BUILT LIKE THIS?
This model illustrates how the Egyptians may have built the pyramids. Workers unload the stone blocks from boats, then slide them up a long ramp to the top of the pyramid.

Mud-brick ramp is built higher as pyramid grows

Stacks of stone blocks

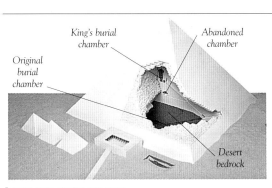

Original burial chamber

King's burial chamber

Abandoned chamber

Desert bedrock

INSIDE THE GREAT PYRAMID
A complex network of passages and dead-end chambers lies within Khufu's pyramid. Workers sealed the shaft leading to the burial chamber with huge blocks of stone.

BUILDING STONES
The pyramid core was made from local limestone. The outer layer – mostly gone now – was high-quality limestone brought by boat from Tura on the east side of the Nile, south of Giza.

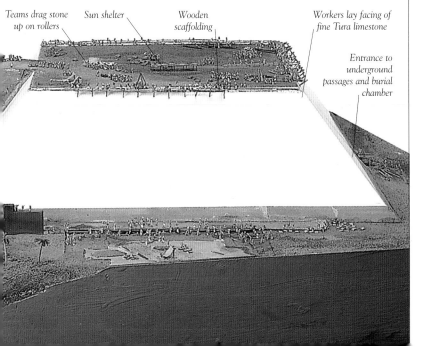

Teams drag stone up on rollers

Sun shelter

Wooden scaffolding

Workers lay facing of fine Tura limestone

Entrance to underground passages and burial chamber

TEMPLES

EGYPTIAN TEMPLES were awesome structures with massive stone walls and rows of columns carved with hieroglyphs and religious images. A temple was the home of a god. Ordinary people could only enter the outer court. In dark rooms at the temple's heart, priests performed sacred rituals.

TEMPLE OF LUXOR
Ramses the Great enlarged this temple and added two obelisks and six colossal statues.

KING-SIZE SCULPTURE
Sculptors used wooden scaffolding to carve the towering statues of kings. Only the pharaoh could be shown as large as the gods in temple statues.

SON OF THE SUN GOD
The pharaoh was believed to be the son of sun god Amun. This "Birth Room" at Luxor Temple has a series of carvings that illustrate Amenhotep III's divine birth.

Elevated roof

Papyrus-shaped columns

COLOSSI OF MEMNON
These giant figures are all that is left of the temple of Amenhotep III, the biggest ever built. A stela records that it was "inlaid with gold throughout, its floors paved with silver."

Pictures of gods

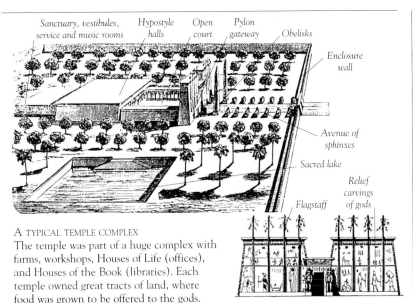

Sanctuary, vestibules, service and music rooms

Hypostyle halls

Open court

Pylon gateway

Obelisks

Enclosure wall

Avenue of sphinxes

Sacred lake

Relief carvings of gods

Flagstaff

A TYPICAL TEMPLE COMPLEX
The temple was part of a huge complex with farms, workshops, Houses of Life (offices), and Houses of the Book (libraries). Each temple owned great tracts of land, where food was grown to be offered to the gods.

PYLON GATEWAY
People entered the temple through a pylon gateway, which was often flanked with seated statues and obelisks. High above, on wooden flagstaffs, flew the gods' flags.

Hall contained 134 columns

HYPOSTYLE HALL AT KARNAK TEMPLE
This powerful temple owned land all over Egypt, and its priests virtually ruled the country at several periods. This is a reconstruction of Karnak's Great Hypostyle Hall. A temple symbolized the creation of the world, which is why the hall's cluster of columns were shaped like plants.

CRAFTS

IN LARGE WORKSHOPS, skilled craftsmen made pots, carved wood to make mummy cases and furniture, cured hides to produce leather, and worked metal and glass to make jewelry and everyday items such as magic amulets, tools, bowls, and even early drainpipes.

Glazed with bright pattern

STRIPED GLASS VESSEL
Glass beads were made before the pharaohs. But glass was not mass-produced until c.1400 B.C. The glass was not blown, so vessels were uneven.

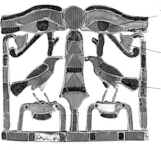

Wadjet eyes

Lotus flower

Birds

Antelope's head

GOLD PECTORAL
The finest jewelry was made in royal workshops. This gold pectoral – a large pendant worn on the chest – is inlaid with gemstones and colored glass.

IVORY ANTELOPE
From predynastic times, the Egyptians used ivory from elephants and hippos to carve a variety of everyday objects. These carvings were often shaped to fit the cylindrical shape of the tusk or tooth. This skillfully crafted toilet dish was made in about 1300 B.C.

POTTERY WORKSHOP
By Old Kingdom times, pots were being made on potters' wheels. After a few days drying in the sun, pots were smoothed and then fired in kilns.

FORMING
LIP OF CUP

SHAPING
OUTER SURFACE

CUTTING CUP
FROM CLAY BASE

STARTING
A NEW CUP

GOLD HAWK
Metals were smelted over an open fire. Before the New Kingdom, when bellows were invented, rows of men stoked the fire by blowing down pipes. The liquid metal was poured into a mold, cooled, and beaten into shape. Dipping in liquid gold was one way to gild objects.

Feather detail

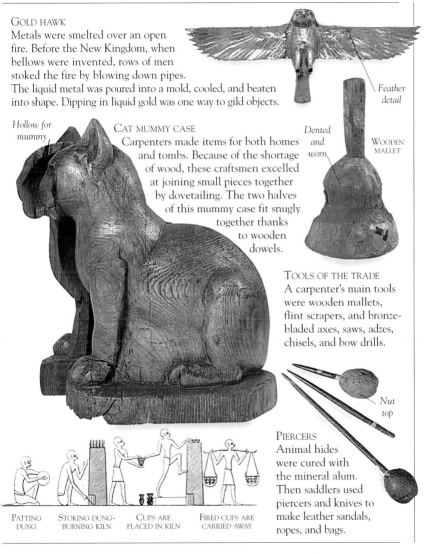

Hollow for mummy

CAT MUMMY CASE
Carpenters made items for both homes and tombs. Because of the shortage of wood, these craftsmen excelled at joining small pieces together by dovetailing. The two halves of this mummy case fit snugly together thanks to wooden dowels.

Dented and worn

WOODEN MALLET

TOOLS OF THE TRADE
A carpenter's main tools were wooden mallets, flint scrapers, and bronze-bladed axes, saws, adzes, chisels, and bow drills.

Nut top

PIERCERS
Animal hides were cured with the mineral alum. Then saddlers used piercers and knives to make leather sandals, ropes, and bags.

PATTING DUNG

STOKING DUNG-BURNING KILN

CUPS ARE PLACED IN KILN

FIRED CUPS ARE CARRIED AWAY

EGYPTIAN ART

THE BEAUTIFUL ART of ancient Egypt was produced by teams of anonymous painters and sculptors. They worked in tombs, temples, palaces, and houses. Their art is highly stylized; figures are almost always depicted in formal poses, and it is difficult to recognize individuals because most subjects are given perfect features.

Artists used grids to calculate "divine proportions"

GRIDLINES
Artists began by drawing a grid. Then they sketched in figures and objects, scaled up from examples in pattern books. Master designers checked and made corrections before work began.

PERIOD STYLES
Each period had its own distinctive artistic style. The art of the Amarna period is dramatically different. This statue of King Akhenaten has the heavy hips and long, oddly distorted face that are typical of the time.

IN A PAINTER'S WORKSHOP
Painters worked on wooden panels or straight onto statues or walls. They applied the paint in flat blocks of color, with no shading or gradations of tone.

SOME CHARACTERISTICS OF EGYPTIAN ART

Artists portrayed everything in its most recognizable form. For example, the human body was shown in profile, but the eyes and chest were face forward. Hieroglyphs were like a caption to the picture.

SKETCHING

Artists worked out ideas with scale models or rough sketches on ostraca (fragments of stone or broken pottery).

ART FACTS

• Tools and paints were so precious that foremen issued them each morning and locked them away at night.

• Fragments of a gigantic statue were found at Tanis. The big toe is the size of a man.

MUMMY CASE

The imagery of religious art had deep meaning to the Egyptians. The gods and symbols painted on mummy cases and tombs were to help the dead avoid the dangers of the underworld.

93

Sculpture and carvings

Ancient Egypt was rich in stone, and sculpture was the most important artform. Copper or bronze tools were used to carve softer materials like limestone and fine woods. These could then be coated with a plaster mixture called *gesso* and painted in bright colors. Hard stone, such as granite, was carved with pounders made of stone. Metal was cast or else beaten into shape.

RAISED RELIEF
This is an example of raised relief, in which the background is cut away to leave the figures raised above the surface.

Ready for crown

Drawn guidelines

SUNK RELIEF
In sunk relief, the outlines of the figures are first gouged out. Then the details within each figure are modeled at various depths. This is a sunk relief of Pharaoh Thutmose III (c.1450 B.C.).

THE FACE OF QUEEN NEFERTITI
Unfinished statues give us many clues about the way sculptors worked. This half-finished bust, marked with guidelines, was found in the ruins of a workshop in the abandoned city of Amarna.

TWO HEADS OF KING USERKAF

Each stone has its own qualities, making it suitable for certain purposes. Here are two heads of the same king. The colossal one is carved in granite, the smaller one in schist.

Pink speckled Aswan granite

GRANITE PHARAOH

Kings' statues were usually carved from hard stone, as they were made to last. This 3,500-year-old granite statue of King Sobkemsaf proves that they did.

LOST WAX METHOD

This bronze figure of King Thutmose IV was made by the lost wax method. The figure was modeled in beeswax. This was then coated in clay and heated until the wax melted. Finally, liquid metal was poured into the clay mold.

Eyes are set in copper

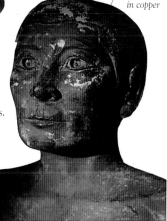

LOOKING LIFELIKE

Some statues have inset eyes. This man's eyes are made from calcite with brown obsidian irises. The effect is so lifelike that the eyes seem to follow you around a room. This is the head of the seated scribe, shown on page 61.

RELIGION

WORSHIP AND BELIEFS

LIKE OTHER ANCIENT PEOPLE, Egyptians believed that all events were controlled by the gods. By wearing amulets (lucky charms) and giving offerings to the gods, the Egyptians hoped for a happy life. They also hoped the gods would help them to live on after death.

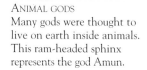

ANIMAL GODS
Many gods were thought to live on earth inside animals. This ram-headed sphinx represents the god Amun.

PROTECTED BY THE GODS
This mummy case is covered in images of gods and magic symbols meant to help the dead person in the afterlife. A Greek wrote that Egyptians were "religious beyond measure, more than any other nation."

Spell for the soul of the dead person

Tomb

Mummy is made ready for the tomb

REPRESENTING THE PHARAOH
The gods were kept happy by priests, who made offerings and conducted rituals in the name of the pharaoh, the sun god's representative on earth. Here, priests perform rights to help the dead person achieve eternal life.

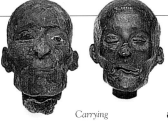

THREE MUMMIFIED HEADS
To live forever, Egyptians had to have their bodies, especially their faces, preserved in a life-like way. This way the spirit of a dead person could recognize its body when it returned to the tomb.

Carrying pole

Servant with fan

CARRIED AWAY
A rich man was buried with this model of a sedan chair carried by three porters. He expected them to come to life after his tomb was sealed.

FACTS ABOUT RELIGION

• The sacred Apis Bull was treated like a god, kept in a luxurious part of the temple, fed the best food, and buried like a pharaoh when it died.

• Many Egyptians were buried with 365 *shabti* figures – one to help on each day of the year.

VIEW OF HEAVEN
In the ideal world shown on his funerary stela, Iy smells flowers with his family. The stela would keep his name alive as he lived these scenes in the afterlife.

MYTHS AND LEGENDS

THE EGYPTIAN CREATION STORY has many versions – most begin in an ocean of chaos. There were hundreds of other myths and legends. But because everyone knew the stories, they were never written down, and few have survived. Luckily, the story of god-king Osiris and his victory over death was recorded by a Greek writer.

ATUM

IN THE BEGINNING
One creation myth tells of a time when Nun, the eternal ocean, filled the universe. When the waters subsided, a primeval hill appeared, on which stood the creator god – the sun god Atum.

Isis nurses the infant Horus, her son by Osiris

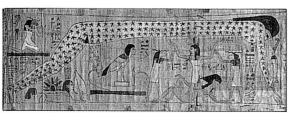

THE GODS ARE CREATED
Atum's children, Shu (air) and Tefnut (moisture), created Geb (earth) and Nut (sky). At first Geb and Nut were joined, but Shu came between them – so separating heaven and earth. Geb and Nut had four children – Osiris, Seth, Isis, and Nephthys.

ISIS AND HORUS
Osiris became king and took sister Isis as his queen. Jealous brother Seth killed Osiris and cut up the body. Isis collected the pieces and made them into the first mummy. Osiris lived on as god of the underworld.

Corn, not
a body,
fills the
bandages

Wadjet Eye
amulets were
placed on
mummies

WADJET EYE

When he grew up, Horus set out to avenge his father's death. Eventually, he vanquished Seth and took the throne. But in their many fights he lost an eye. This Eye of Horus, or *Wadjet* Eye, became a symbol of victory over evil.

MURDER OF A BROTHER

Seth held a banquet where he showed off a beautiful casket, saying he would give it to whoever fit inside. When Osiris climbed in, Seth locked it and threw it in the Nile. Isis found the casket, but Seth seized it and cut up Osiris' body.

SACRED SHAPES

According to legend, the rays of the sun fell first of all upon the primeval mound, or *ben-ben*. This sacred shape was recreated in obelisks and may have been the reason for the structure of pyramids.

SUN TEMPLE

OSIRIS

This is a corn mummy in the shape of Osiris. At first he was a fertility god, responsible for the floods that brought new life to Egypt every year. As the first king to survive death, he became a god of rebirth.

101

THE SUN GODS

SOURCE OF ALL HEAT AND LIGHT, the sun was worshipped from earliest times. This life-giving force took many forms, each represented by a different god or personality. The rising sun was a scarab beetle; at noon it was Ra, the orange disc itself; while in the evening it took the form of a ram. Satirical literary texts depict the setting sun as a dribbling, decrepit old man.

AMUN-RA
During the New Kingdom, power moved to Thebes in the south. Theban priests merged their local god Amun, a creator god, with the powerful sun god Ra. Throughout the land, Egyptians worshipped Amun-Ra as chief god.

Akhenaten and his family worship Aten

AKHENATEN, THE SUN KING
To break the power of the Theban priesthood, King Amenhotep IV banned all gods but Aten, the sun in its purest form. It was depicted as a disc with rays that touched with human hands. The king changed his name to Akhenaten and built a new city dedicated to Aten at Amarna.

WINGED SCARAB

The scarab is a beetle that rolls up balls of dung to lay its eggs inside. Egyptians believed that a giant scarab made the sun in the same way and then rolled it over the horizon and across the sky.

Scarab god clasps the sun in its claws

Prayers to the sun god

SAILING THROUGH THE NIGHT

When the sun set in the West, the Egyptians believed it sailed through the underworld on a boat before rising again in the East. Here, the god Nun steers the boat safely through the waters of chaos.

IMHOTEP

The cult of the sun began at Heliopolis. Here, King Djoser's chief minister Imhotep designed the first pyramid – possibly as a stairway, so the dead pharaoh could join the sun god in the sky.

SUN STRUCK

Heliopolis means "Sun City." In its temple, priests kept a triangular stone, the *ben-ben* – believed to be the first object struck by the sun's rays when the world was created. This tomb cap is carved in the same magical shape.

RA-HARAKHTY

Sun gods are usually depicted with the disc of the sun on their heads. The god on the far right is Ra-Harakhty, a falcon-headed sun god and a version of the sky god Horus.

103

GODS AND GODDESSES

EGYPTIANS HAD A DIZZYING number of gods – one ancient text lists 740. But only a small number were worshipped in the same place at the same time. All the forces of nature were represented by gods or goddesses. Temples were dedicated to state gods or important local deities and controlled by an elite priesthood. Ordinary people were excluded.

Ptah is depicted with a tight skull cap pulled over his shaven head

Flail

PTAH
The cult center of this god was Memphis, capital city during the Old Kingdom. By New Kingdom times, Ptah had become a state god. He is always shown as a man, wrapped up like a mummy. He was a creator god and a patron of craftsmen.

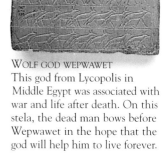

WOLF GOD WEPWAWET
This god from Lycopolis in Middle Egypt was associated with war and life after death. On this stela, the dead man bows before Wepwawet in the hope that the god will help him to live forever.

MIN
The fertility god Min wears two tall plumes on his hat and holds a flail – an agricultural tool. One of his symbols was lettuce, which the Egyptians considered a fertility food.

MAAT

The basic laws of the universe – justice, truth, and order – were represented by the goddess Maat. Her name meant "straight." She wore the *Feather of Truth* on her head. Maat is often shown as a doll, held by the sun god Ra.

Palette and pen

HATHOR

Some gods had different roles in different parts of Egypt. Hathor, goddess of love, music, and dance, was shown as a woman or a cow. In the Delta, she was associated with the sky and held the sun between her horns. In Thebes, she was a goddess of death.

KHNUM

This ram-headed creator god is sometimes shown molding people on a potter's wheel. At Aswan, Khnum was guardian of the Nile and worshipped as "he who brought the flood."

THOTH

Many gods were associated with animals. For example, Thoth, the god of writing and wisdom, was depicted as an ibis – a bird that the Egyptians thought was wise. Here he is shown as an ibis-headed man writing with a scribe's pen and palette.

BASTET

Worship of the cat goddess Bastet began at Bubastis, in the Delta. In later times she became popular all over Egypt, and her annual festival was a national celebration.

105

MAGIC AND POPULAR RELIGION

THE STATE GODS played little part in normal life. If they had a sick child or a son at war, Egyptians asked protection from more down-to-earth gods. People wore amulets (lucky charms) and recited prayers and spells to ward off disease or disaster.

Taweret was shown as a pregnant hippo

OFFERING SHRINE

Like most ancient people, the Egyptians tried to please the gods by giving offerings of food and drink. They did this at temples, in chapels set up next to tombs, or in small shrines inside the home.

Lotus-bud shape

BES

Part dwarf and part lion, Bes was a popular household god. He carried a knife and a musical instrument, whose sweet sounds warded off bad spirits.

TAWERET

Childbirth was dangerous, both for the mother and the baby. Egyptians prayed and put their faith in Taweret, the goddess of childbirth.

MAGIC WAND

This magical stick was made from a hippo tusk. It is carved with powerful symbols, and it could be used to create a defensive barrier around a part of the house. These wands were also used to protect a child or a sick person.

MEDICAL TOOLS
Egyptians believed in magic, but they were also highly skilled at medicine. This temple carving shows a range of medical instruments, including forceps. One papyrus lists over 700 prescriptions for different ailments, grouped according to the sick organ.

HOUSE CHARM
This stela asks god Horus to protect the family from the dangers of daily life. He tramples on two crocodiles and grips snakes, lions, and scorpions in his hands. Above Horus' head, Bes pokes his tongue out at evil spirits. Magic spells cover the stela's sides.

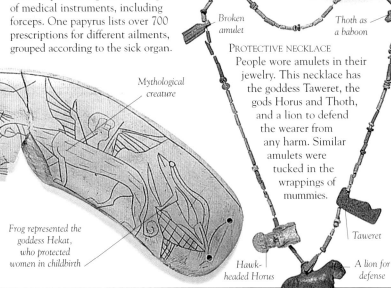

Mythological creature

Frog represented the goddess Hekat, who protected women in childbirth

Broken amulet

Thoth as a baboon

PROTECTIVE NECKLACE
People wore amulets in their jewelry. This necklace has the goddess Taweret, the gods Horus and Thoth, and a lion to defend the wearer from any harm. Similar amulets were tucked in the wrappings of mummies.

Taweret

Hawk-headed Horus

A lion for defense

PRIESTS AND RITUALS

ANCIENT EGYPTIAN PRIESTS were called "servants of the gods." Their job was not to preach to the people, but to keep the gods happy and fulfilled. They did this by performing elaborate rituals in the sacred inner sanctums of temples, where only senior priests and the pharaoh were allowed to enter.

Cup for burning incense

PURE ONE
To show their purity, priests shaved their heads and bodies and washed many times a day. This man burns incense and sprinkles water from the sacred lake. In the inner sanctum of the temple, the priest chanted "I am a Pure One" as he approached the gold statue of the god.

Hair in sidelock of youth

Offering table

Bucket held water from sacred lake

CHILD PRIEST
There were many different classes of priests. This one wears his hair in a sidelock of youth, not because of his age, but to show that he is acting as the loving son of the god.

SITULA
(SACRED
BUCKET)

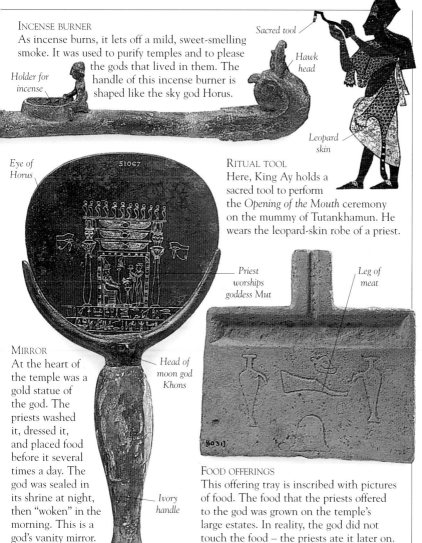

INCENSE BURNER

As incense burns, it lets off a mild, sweet-smelling smoke. It was used to purify temples and to please the gods that lived in them. The handle of this incense burner is shaped like the sky god Horus.

Holder for incense

Sacred tool

Hawk head

Leopard skin

RITUAL TOOL

Here, King Ay holds a sacred tool to perform the *Opening of the Mouth* ceremony on the mummy of Tutankhamun. He wears the leopard-skin robe of a priest.

Eye of Horus

51067

Priest worships goddess Mut

Leg of meat

MIRROR

At the heart of the temple was a gold statue of the god. The priests washed it, dressed it, and placed food before it several times a day. The god was sealed in its shrine at night, then "woken" in the morning. This is a god's vanity mirror.

Head of moon god Khons

Ivory handle

FOOD OFFERINGS

This offering tray is inscribed with pictures of food. The food that the priests offered to the god was grown on the temple's large estates. In reality, the god did not touch the food – the priests ate it later on.

109

DEATH AND BURIAL

THE EGYPTIANS WANTED TO LIVE forever. To achieve this, they believed that a dead person's body had to be preserved, or "mummified." The mummy was then buried with elaborate rites and a book of magic spells to help it in its journey through the treacherous underworld.

Pieces of gold leaf

GIRL MUMMY
This is the body of a girl who died over 2,000 years ago, aged eight or nine. Her body was coated in oils and resins to stop it from decaying and then covered in gold leaf – maybe because Ra, the sun god, was believed to have a skin of gold.

Ba *bird*   Mummy

THE MUMMY'S SOUL
Egyptians believed that a person's spirit took several forms. One of these was the Ba, similar to a soul. The Ba – depicted as a bird – left the body at death. Only when it returned would the person live forever.

TOMB OWNERS

Statues of the dead were placed in the tomb chapel to make sure that the gods knew who was buried there. Loved ones visited the chapel to put offerings before the statues.

A HUMBLE HEAVEN

The Egyptians' idea of heaven was a rural paradise, presided over by the god Osiris. They called it the *Field of Reeds* – a place where the sun shone and people worked in the fields, planting and harvesting their crops. In fact, it was just like Egypt – except grain grew a foot taller.

Husband and wife

ANUBIS

The god of death and embalming was the jackal-headed Anubis. He was thought to guard mummies and necropolises (burial grounds). A priest wearing an Anubis mask supervised the ritual practices that surrounded the process of embalming (preserving).

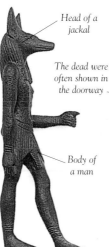

Head of a jackal

The dead were often shown in the doorway

Body of a man

FALSE DOOR

Tomb walls contained false doors – gateways between the worlds of the living and the dead. The spirits of the dead were thought to come and go through these doorways.

FUNERAL PROCESSION

Mourners wailed and splashed their faces with mud, as priests dragged the mummy to the tomb. Before sealing the mummy in, the priests performed sacred rites and repeated magic spells.

PREPARING A MUMMY

TO STOP IT FROM ROTTING away, a body was preserved by embalming. After the internal organs were removed, the corpse was washed, dried out with natural salts, and then coated with oils and resins. Finally, it was wrapped in many layers of tight linen bandages. The whole process took 70 days.

PROTECTIVE EYE
Cuts made in the flesh were covered with plates like this one. It bears a sacred symbol, the Eye of Horus, to protect the body.

RITUAL KNIVES
The internal organs were removed through an incision cut in the abdomen. The brain was drawn out with a hook passed through the nose.

Duamutef guarded the stomach

CANOPIC JARS
Intestines, lungs, stomach, and liver were mummified separately and put in four canopic jars. The lids depicted gods, who stopped evil forces using the organs in spells against the dead.

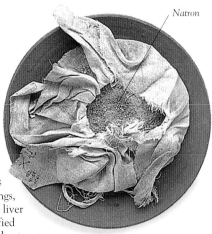

Natron

PRESERVING SALT
To stop decay, a body must be thoroughly dried out. The Egyptians did this with dry crystals of natron, a natural salt found by desert lakes. The procedure took 40 days.

KEEPING HER HAIR
This skull of a woman is 3,500 years old. Skin and flesh have rotted away, leaving nothing but hair and bone. Every hair was saved and then placed in the tomb, because a lost strand could be used in spells against her.

Plaited hair

Teeth can give clues about age and diet

Linen bandages

MUMMY OF A BOY
A mummy could be wrapped in more than 20 layers of bandages. As each one was added, it was brushed with oils and resins.

OPENING THE MOUTH
During mummification, there were constant prayers and rituals. The most important was the *Opening of the Mouth*, held just before burial. It was meant to restore the mummy's senses.

WRAPPED UP
Before wrapping, the dried body was stuffed with linen and sawdust to restore shape. Sunken cheeks might be padded out and artificial eyes put in.

MUMMY LABEL
Embalming was done by special priests. They made sure body parts were not mixed up by tying labels to the mummies.

113

JOURNEY TO THE AFTERLIFE

TO REACH HEAVEN, the Egyptians believed that a dead person had to travel through *Duat*, the underworld, where monsters and lakes of fire awaited. To fight them, the mummy was forearmed with a collection of magic spells, written in the *Book of the Dead*. The book included a map of *Duat* and many prayers to ward off evil.

BOX OF WORKERS
Shabtis are model workers placed in the tomb. They are inscribed with Chapter Six of the *Book of the Dead*.

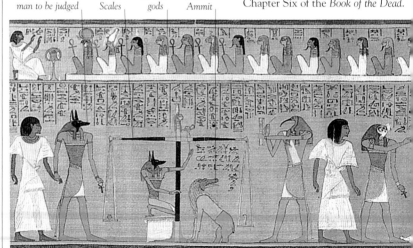

Anubis takes dead man to be judged   Scales   Jury of gods   Monster Ammit

STILL TALKING

This tomb model of a man and wife chatting shows how Egyptians expected life to be much the same after death. They crammed their tombs with jewelry, clothes, food, games, makeup, and anything else they might need in the afterlife.

Ptah-Sokar-Osiris wearing Atef *crown and false beard*

Base of statue

Scroll

EXTRA PROTECTION

Amulets – magic charms worn like jewelry or put into the wrappings – also helped protect a mummy from evil. The *djed* pillar was thought to give strength.

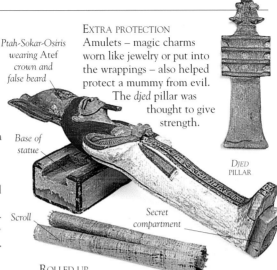

DJED PILLAR

Secret compartment

ROLLED UP

The Book of the Dead was written on scrolls of papyrus and put in the tomb. This statue of composite god Ptah-Sokar-Osiris has a hidden compartment where the scroll was kept.

Osiris, god of the underworld, presides over judgment

Goddess Nephthys with sister Isis

WEIGHING THE HEART

The final test came in the *Hall of the Two Truths*. Here, Anubis weighed the dead person's heart to see if it was heavy with sin. If it was lighter than the *Feather of Truth*, the person lived forever. If not, the heart was thrown to the monster Ammit, "Devourer of the Dead."

HEART PROTECTOR

Pectorals are amulets that were laid on the mummy's chest to guard the heart, a symbol of life. Many were inscribed with pleas such as "See, this heart of mine, it weeps and pleads for mercy."

MUMMY CASES

THE FINISHED MUMMY was laid in a coffin, or mummy case. Like the tomb, this case was seen as a "house" for the dead person's spirit. Mummy cases changed gradually through the course of history, but from the earliest days the Egyptians covered them with magic symbols and pleas to the gods.

WOODEN CASE
For a long time, all mummy cases were wooden. In later times, many inner cases were made of cheaper materials – layers of papyrus or linen, pressed together like papier mâché.

Mummy was sealed inside while cartonnage was still wet

LACED IN TIGHT
Many mummies were buried in two or three cases – one inside the other like Russian dolls. The tight-fitting inner case was laced up at the back.

Reed matting tied with twine ropes

MASKED MUMMY
This mummy of a woman is wearing a painted mask over her head and shoulders. She is also decked out in a wide selection of protective amulets.

BABY COFFIN
The earliest coffins, from about 3000 B.C., were simple reed baskets. This later example (c.1400 B.C.) contains the body of a baby. Bone deformities indicate death due to serious illness.

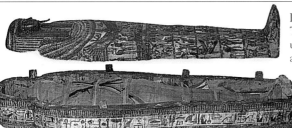

LOOKING GOOD
The mummy case
usually presented
an idealized portrait of
the dead person.
Analysis of this
youthful-looking
mummy shows
that he was about
50 when he died.

FACTORY FACE
This is a wooden portrait
from a coffin. Sometimes
the face was made separately
and pegged onto the case.
These carved features
were often mass produced.
Regional styles allow experts
to identify the area of Egypt.

SAFELY INSIDE
The priests in charge of embalming
secure a mummy in its case. Wooden
cases were held together
with thick pegs.

WOODEN BOX
A pharaoh or
an important
official had an
extra stone coffin,
or sarcophagus.
These massive
structures were
extremely heavy
and difficult to
move. This priest
(Hor) had an
extra wooden
box instead.

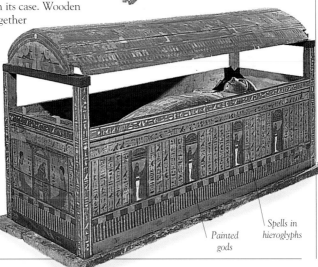

*Painted
gods*

*Spells in
hieroglyphs*

Animal mummies

Beetles, birds, cats, crocodiles – the Egyptians mummified an amazing array of creatures. Some were beloved household pets. But most animals were mummified because of their association with particular gods. In later times, millions of animals were bred just to be mummified and buried in special cemeteries dedicated to the gods. Four million ibis mummies were found in one cemetery, each in its own pot.

Painted face

Geometric wrappings, a feature of the Roman period

IBIS
This large wading bird is still common in the marshes by the Nile. It was sacred to Thoth, the god of writing and wisdom and patron of scribes.

Biologists have used mummies and ancient pictures of ibises to show that the species has not changed in 5,000 years.

CAT MUMMY
Egyptians were the first people to keep cats as pets. The earliest written mention dates from 2100 B.C. They probably tamed African wild cats, a species that was the ancestor of all modern pets. Cats were linked with goddess Bastet.

Anubis, god of embalming

FOUR FALCONS
The falcon was king of the Egyptian skies and was seen as a representative of the sky god Horus. This case contains four falcon mummies and is painted with funerary scenes.

Carved falcon, symbol of the sky god Horus

UNWRAPPED CROCODILE
Crocodiles were sacred to the water god Sobek. Priests kept pet crocodiles in luxury, feeding them on the best meat and wines.

Ears are flattened against skull

Fur

PRESERVED FISH
Other animals found as mummies include fish, vultures, owls, baboons, rats, snakes, mice, dogs, geese, scarab beetles, shrews, lizards, rams, and huge bulls.

UNDER THE LINEN
The legs of this unwrapped cat mummy have been tucked in to make a compact shape. Many of these cats were bred by priests just to be mummified and sold to worshippers visiting the temples.

Case has door at back

Each case contained a cat mummy

Tail curled up between legs

CAT CASES
These cat mummy cases all come from Bubastis, sacred city of Bastet. In later times, the festival of Bastet was an important yearly event. Huge celebrations were held in honor of the goddess, and hunting lions was forbidden.

119

VALLEY OF THE KINGS

DURING THE NEW KINGDOM, the capital city moved to Thebes in the south, and pharaohs were buried in the desolate Valley of the Kings. These royal tombs were hidden, cut deep into the rock. Steep steps and cramped passages led to the burial chamber, where the pharaoh's mummy lay surrounded by fabulous treasures.

VALLEY VIEW
The ancient Egyptians called the Valley of the Kings *The Great Place*. Neighboring Valley of the Queens was known as *The Place of Beauty*. This view across the Nile shows the temple of Queen Hatshepsut.

OVERSEER
The workers who built the kings' tombs lived in the nearby village of Deir el-Medina. A few, like the overseer Sennedjem, had beautifully painted tombs.

STAR-STUDDED CEILING
The Egyptians decorated tomb walls with exquisite paintings and reliefs. This is their view of the northern sky at night, from Sety I's tomb. Animals represent constellations, which are named in heiroglyphs.

Red spots represent bright stars

Egyptians could tell the time from the position of constellations

TOMB OF RAMSES IX
This pharaoh tried accused tomb robbers. One confessed "We took gold and jewels and the precious metal of his coffins. Then we found the queen and took everything that was hers and set fire to the coffins."

VALLEY TODAY
In ancient times, the valley was guarded. In spite of this, thieves had looted almost every tomb by 1000 B.C. Today, tombs in the valley are threatened by ground water, pollution, and endless crowds of tourists.

MAN AT WORK
This sketch shows a bald, unshaven mason using a chisel and mallet. Building the tombs was hot, thirsty work.

The Egyptians called this constellation Mes

Crocodile rides on hippo's back

The sun disk

Tutankhamun's tomb

In 1922, the English archaeologist Howard Carter found the tomb of a little known pharaoh, buried 3,200 years earlier in the Valley of the Kings. Crammed inside were priceless treasures that amazed the world. As Carter said, "There were rooms full of gold, everywhere the glint of gold."

Crook and flail, symbols of the pharaoh's power

Squatting baboon gods

INNER COFFIN
The dead pharaoh was buried in three mummy cases, one inside another. The outer two shine with gold leaf, but the inner case is made from solid gold and inlaid with gemstones. This coffin weighs an incredible 245 lb (110 kg).

BURIAL CHAMBER
The outer coffin has now been returned to the stone sarcophagus in Tutankhamun's burial chamber. The walls are painted with gods and scenes from the underworld.

SHRINE DETAIL
The sarcophagus was housed in four wooden shrines, fitting one inside another. All four glittered with gold-leaf decoration.

MUMMY MASK
The most famous treasure is the portrait mask, which covered the pharaoh's head as he lay in state. He wears a falcon-headed collar, false beard, and striped *nemes* headdress. Made from solid gold inlaid with gemstones, this masterpiece weighs 22.5 lb (10.2 kg).

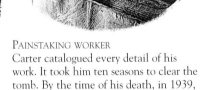

PAINSTAKING WORKER
Carter catalogued every detail of his work. It took him ten seasons to clear the tomb. By the time of his death, in 1939, he had published three volumes of notes.

MUMMY
The king's mummy was inside his inner coffin. In separate miniature coffins were two tiny mummies, probably his stillborn twin daughters.

THE GOLDEN THRONE
This is made of carved wood inlaid with intricate designs. The back panel shows the king and his wife.

PILED HIGH
Here, the throne can be seen as it was found. The tomb's four rooms were piled high with treasures. It had been prepared in a hurry, probably because the king died suddenly. Later the entrance was blocked by accident, so the tomb was forgotten for more than 3,000 years.

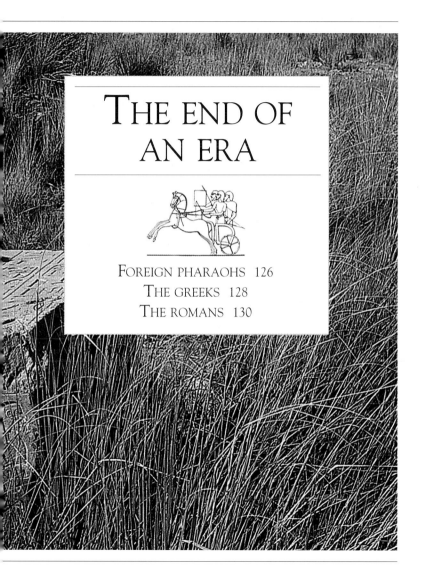

THE END OF AN ERA

FOREIGN PHARAOHS

THE SPLENDORS of the New Kingdom ended with the death of Ramses XI in 1069 B.C. The empire was gone, and Egypt was once again split by war and chaos. In the centuries that followed, the country was invaded by its powerful neighbors. Egyptian culture still thrived, but life by the Nile was not as stable.

POWERFUL PRIESTS
The priests of Amun at Karnak Temple near Thebes became so powerful that they were able to challenge the authority of the pharaoh. This helped lead to the collapse of the New Kingdom.

TEMPLE OF AMUN AT KARNAK

CAPTIVE ENEMY
Egypt's traditional enemies came from what is now the Middle East. They included Babylonians, Hyksos, Hittites, and the Persians, who ruled Egypt twice (525–359 and 343–332 B.C.).

LIBYAN MUMMY
This is the mummy case of a Libyan called Pasenhor. Many Libyans settled in the Delta, and their chiefs ruled Egypt from 945 to 715 B.C. The Libyan pharaohs were resident kings, who wrote in Egyptian scripts and worshipped Egyptian gods.

CAT WORSHIP
The Libyan kings moved their northern capital from Tanis to Bubastis, city of cat goddess Bastet. She became one of the most popular Egyptian gods and was worshipped all over Egypt.

STRONG NEIGHBORS
For many centuries, Egypt was the only great power. But its neighbors developed and, one by one, they overran its borders. Libyan and Nubian kings lived like native Egyptians, but Assyria and Persia ruled Egypt as a colony.

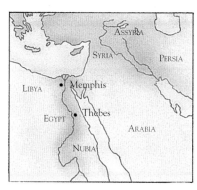

NUBIAN KING
This is Taharqo, one of the Nubian kings. They ruled Egypt from 747 to 656 B.C. Their empire was bigger than Egypt at its height.

Egyptian gods

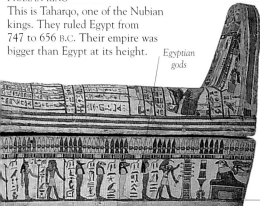

FACTS ABOUT THE ERA

• The Nubian pharaohs were buried in pyramids in the desert of Sudan.

• The Persians introduced the camel.

• According to legend, Alexander the Great was mummified and laid in a glass coffin floating in honey. It has never been found.

THE GREEKS

ALEXANDER THE GREAT conquered Egypt in 332 B.C. He built a new capital city, Alexandria, on the coast. When he died, his general Ptolemy founded a dynasty that ruled Egypt for 300 years. The new rulers spoke Greek and followed Greek law. But they respected the local culture, which continued to flourish.

TEMPLE OF ISIS AT PHILAE
The Greeks built many great temples in Egypt, dedicated to the Egyptian gods. On the walls, the Ptolemies were shown as pharaohs. But these Greek rulers rarely left Alexandria on the Mediterranean coast, and there were regular revolts against them.

ALEXANDER THE GREAT (356–323 B.C)
This great war leader was born in Macedonia, part of the Greek empire. Shortly after he became king, at age 20, he conquered the entire Persian empire, including Egypt, Syria, and Mesopotamia. His huge empire broke up after he died suddenly of a fever.

FOUR DIFFERENT SCRIPTS

Greek became the official language under the Ptolemies. Hieroglyphs were only used for religious inscriptions; priests wrote in demotic. Many documents were still written in hieratic. This detail from the Rosetta Stone shows the same text in Greek and demotic.

GREEK MUMMY MASK

The invaders adopted many local traditions. The mix of Greek and Egyptian art and religion created many new hybrids. This mummy mask has realistic Greek-style features and the headdress of a wealthy Egyptian.

Lotus flowers

Greek-style sculpture of an Egyptian icon

Body of lion

CLEOPATRA FROM TEMPLE OF HATHOR, DENDERA

ALEXANDRIA

This city became an important cultural center, famous for its lighthouse and library. The library – the greatest in the Classical World – burned down. This sphinx was part of the library complex.

CLEOPATRA VII (69–30 B.C.)

The last Ptolemaic ruler was Cleopatra VII. She tried to save Egypt from the Romans, using her legendary charm to seduce first Julius Caesar and then Mark Anthony. But, when Roman general Octavian invaded Egypt in 30 B.C., she killed herself.

129

THE ROMANS

EGYPT BECAME A ROMAN state after the conquest by Octavian in 30 B.C. The Roman capital was Alexandria, but the emperors ruled from Rome and took little interest in local traditions. Not surprisingly, there were regular uprisings. In A.D. 642, Egypt was invaded by Muslim armies.

AUGUSTUS (63 B.C.–A.D. 14)
Octavian, Egypt's conqueror, became Emperor Augustus Caesar. He made Egypt the granary of Rome, forcing the country to export huge quantities of wheat to feed the rest of the Roman empire.

Real rings

MUMMY CASE
Mummification of the dead continued under the Romans. Some mummy cases show the dead person dressed in their best clothes. This Roman woman is wearing a colorful toga, sandals, and wig. Her jewelry even includes real gold rings.

PORTRAIT
During Roman times, a portrait, painted on a wooden panel, was often put over the face of the dead person and secured by bandages. Painted from life, this portrait may have hung in the house until the sitter died.

GOLD PARTS
Shaped pieces of gold leaf were placed over tongues, eyes, and other body parts of Roman mummies in the belief that these would restore the various functions in the afterlife.

Bunch of flowers

Gold tongue to allow mummy to speak

MUMMY MASK
This Roman mummy mask is probably one of many made in a factory from an original model. Typical of the period, he is holding a candle and a bunch of flowers, which are both symbols of rebirth.

HADRIAN (A.D. 76–138)
The only emperor to take much interest in Egypt, Hadrian was fascinated by its culture. He brought these statues back to grace his villa near Rome. He also founded a new city, named Antinoopolis, at the spot by the Nile where his lover drowned.

This area of the villa was inspired by Canopus, an Egyptian town

NILE SCENE
Alexandria was a center of art. Workshops there produced many frescoes and mosaics, which were exported all over the Roman empire. This Nile-scene mosaic comes from a villa in Pompeii, Italy.

Pair of ducks   *Crocodile*   *Songbird on water plant*   *Ibis*

131

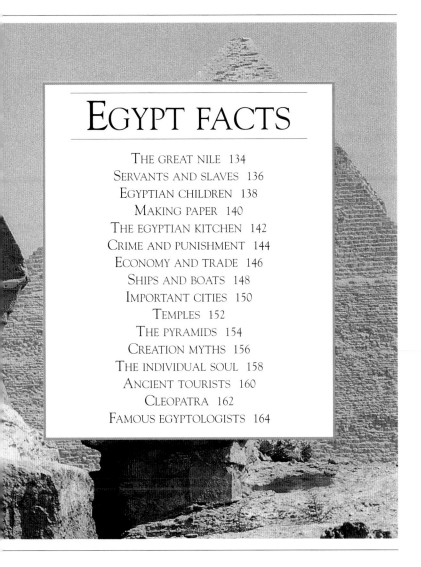

EGYPT FACTS

THE GREAT NILE

THE RIVER AND AGRICULTURE

Almost every aspect of life in ancient Egypt was affected by the annual inundation (flood) of the Nile, the longest river in the world.

- The White Nile, the Blue Nile, and the Atbara (in present-day Sudan) all flow into the Nile (which was called Iteru in ancient Egypt).

- The Nile divided into seven channels in the Delta (the most fertile part of ancient Egypt) before it flowed into the Mediterranean Sea.

- Floodwaters began to rise in June at 1.5–3 in (4–8 cm) per day, and deposited silt (rich muddy soil) on the land.

- The calendar was divided into three seasons that corresponded to the phases of the river – the flood season, the growing season, and the drought season.

THE NILOMETER

Nilometers were associated with temples, and fulfilled a mainly religious function. Priests divined the will of the gods according to the Nile tides. Nilometers were huge stone staircases that went down into the river and measured the level of the water and how fast it was rising during the flood. Nilometers still exist at Dendera, Edfu, Esna, Philae, Kom Ombo, in Cairo, and on Elephantine Island at Aswan.

This Nilometer at Elephantine Island, Aswan, was used to measure the depth of the Nile.

THE ASWAN DAM

- The Aswan High Dam, begun in 1960 and opened in 1970, created Lake Nasser, which helped to control the Nile's floodwaters and improve agriculture.

- Many ancient monuments were lost when Lake Nasser was created, and over 60,000 Nubians had to be resettled.

- With the support of UNESCO (United Nations Educational, Scientific, and Cultural Organization), 14 temples and monuments were moved to safety, including Philae, Abu Simbel, and Kalabsha.

- The famous rock-cut temples of Abu Simbel were removed, numbered in pieces, and rebuilt in a safe area.

DAM FACTS

Tranjan's kiosk at the Sanctuary of Isis, in Philae, was saved from the floodwaters by the UNESCO campaign.

- Lake Nasser, created by the Aswan Dam, is 310 miles (500 km) long, between 6 and 18 miles (10 and 30 km) wide and 295 ft (90 m) deep.
- The dam is 2.5 miles (3.6 km) long and 365 ft (111 m) high.

HOW FARMERS USED THE FLOODWATERS

- Farmers used the floodwaters in two important ways: the flood deposited fertile soil on the land, and it provided the water to grow crops.

- As the floods were subsiding in October or November, farmers captured water in canals, basins, and reservoirs for later use.

- The rich soil, deposited as silt, supported two crops a year, but the second one needed to be watered by hand.

- Crops were watered in a variety of ways. Farmers often carried water in two clay jars slung on a wooden yoke across their shoulders.

- *Shadufs* (buckets on the end of a pole, with a counterweight on the other end) were used during the New Kingdom (c.1550–1086 B.C.).

- *Sakkias* (animal-powered water wheels) lifted water onto the fields in the Greek period (332–30 B.C.).

135

SERVANTS AND SLAVES

WORKERS

- The king, temple officials, and nobles owned most slaves and servants. Servants, unlike slaves, were freeborn, although both often performed the same tasks.

- Servants received food and other goods as payment for their services, but slaves were not paid. They were kept by their masters.

SERFS (SEMEDET)

- Serfs, or farm workers, were freeborn, although most were tied to the land, working for landowners.

- They could own land, but had little opportunity to change their career.

- Each year they were expected to grow a certain amount of grain or other produce, which was handed over as a form of tax.

- During the flood season, farm workers left their fields and livestock to help build the pharaoh's pyramids, temples, and other monuments.

- Punishments were severe for nonpayment of taxes. If the crops failed, the workers were still expected to pay.

DOMESTIC SERVANTS

- Large households and organizations had many servants to perform clearly defined tasks.

- Cooking, cleaning, gardening, child care, weaving, and hundreds of other tasks were done by servants who were paid by the temple, nobles, or the king.

- Middle-class households also had servants or slaves to help with the domestic chores.

- A servant's profession or craft was passed down from father to son and from mother to daughter.

- Servants could leave their master if he was unjust. They were allowed to set up their own business and buy property.

WHO REALLY BUILT THE PYRAMIDS?

- A labor force of thousands of men was needed to build the pyramids.

- Contrary to popular belief, Egypt's pyramids were not built by slaves.

- Most of the workers were farm laborers, who owed their labor as tax and worked on the pyramids when they were not required on the land.

- Prisoners of war and convicts sometimes quarried and mined stone for the pyramids. They were not a significant part of the work force until the Middle (2040–1750 B.C.) and New (1550–1086 B.C.) Kingdoms.

- Artisans such as carpenters, stone masons, sculptors, painters, potters, and cabinet makers also helped.

SLAVE LABOR

- Most slaves (*hemw*) were foreigners, usually prisoners of war from other countries.

- Prisoners of war were given to the king, to a temple, or to soldiers as a reward for their bravery.

- Slaves could be hired out, sold, or exchanged as goods at any time.

- Egyptians sometimes sold themselves into slavery in order to have a home and food to eat.

- Slaves could be freed by their masters. They were given presents and could also own property with their master's consent.

- Slaves could marry someone who was freeborn, which released them from their status as a slave.

FEMALE SLAVES

- Female slaves worked at spinning, weaving, cleaning, and many other domestic chores.

- Beautiful slave women were highly prized and well cared for. They were sold for high prices to temples to become dancers, singers, or servants.

- Ramses II (c.1279–1213 B.C.) is reputed to have branded his female slaves with his name.

Female attendants helping their mistress.

EGYPTIAN CHILDREN

FAMILY LIFE

- Ancient Egyptians had large families – four to seven children on average. They wanted to make sure there would be someone to perform the religious rituals after they died.

- Boys were expected to help their fathers, and girls their mothers.

- Girls stayed at home until they were about 13, when they got married. Boys left home at puberty, when they were considered to be adults.

- Some marriages were arranged, but people often married for love. Divorce was common – proceedings could be begun by husband or wife.

HOW DID THEY DRESS?

- Young children mostly went naked because of the heat.

- Older boys wore a short kilt made of linen. Girls wore a long straight dress.

- Underwear was a simple linen loincloth.

- Most children went barefoot. Sandals were a luxury, or an indication of status.

- Winter clothes were made of wool and heavier linen.

- Like adults, children's eyes were outlined with kohl (a black cosmetic) for decoration, and for protection against the sun and infection.

GAMES AND SPORTS

Egyptian children had plenty of amusements and played many games. Older children played leapfrog, ball games, tug-of-war, and board games, while smaller children had pull-along toys, tops, dolls, and balls. Boys practiced shooting at targets with a bow and arrows, as well as boxing, wrestling, and stick-fighting in preparation for going into the army. Girls were encouraged to do gymnastics, juggling, dancing, and singing. Some children kept pets.

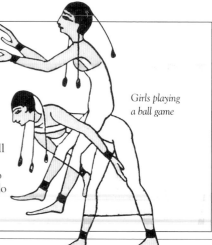

Girls playing a ball game

THE BOY-PHARAOH

- Tutankhamun came to the throne when he was only nine years old and reigned from 1336 to 1327 B.C..
- He died (or was murdered) when he was 18. An X-ray of his mummified body shows damage to the skull, which may have been caused by a blow to the head, a fall, or damage from the mummification process.
- Tutankhamun's tomb is famous because it was found with most of its priceless treasure intact. It still contained more than 200 pieces of jewelry, 16 model boats, furniture, clothes, cosmetics, and food.

Tutankhamun's mask was made of gold and inlaid with precious stones.

- Souvenirs from his boyhood included a board game called senet, a tiny bow with which the pharaoh must have learned to shoot, and miniature tables and chairs.
- It took archaeologist Howard Carter (1874–1939) five years to list all the treasures of Tutankhamun's tomb.

GOING TO SCHOOL

- Education was expensive, and only boys were allowed to attend school.
- Boys who did go to school went at five years of age and carried on into their teens. Boys whose parents couldn't afford school fees worked and learned their fathers' trades.
- Girls never went to school, but some were taught to read and write at home by one of their parents or an older brother. Most girls learned to spin, weave, and cook.
- Education was a way of advancing in Egyptian society. Many people wanted their sons to become scribes.
- Schools were attached to temples and government offices, with priests as teachers.
- Young students learned hieratic script (used by priests). They wrote on wooden boards or broken pieces of pottery, because papyrus paper was too expensive. Students made their own brushes and inks.
- Older students studied hieroglyphics, mathematics, history, languages, geography, astronomy, and law, as well as gymnastics and good manners.

MAKING PAPER

ORIGINS

Our word "paper" comes from the Greek *papyrus*, which is the word for the writing material invented by the Egyptians as well as the reed from which it is made.

- Ancient Egyptians discovered how to make papyrus paper in about 2500 B.C.

- The paper was strong, flexible, white, and very durable.

- Papyrus paper was expensive to produce and was used only for important texts such as archives, accounts, religious writings, and literature.

OTHER WRITING SURFACES

Students wrote on used bits of broken pottery (*ostraca*) because paper was too expensive.

They also wrote on leather, soft stone, and slabs of wood spread with plaster. *Stelae* (stone or wood carved with text, paintings, and reliefs) were used for religious or commemorative purposes.

A cartouche of Ramses II (c.1279–1213 B.C.) from the Temple of Abu Simbel.

THE BOOK OF THE DEAD

- This collection of spells is the most famous Egyptian text. It contains spells for mummification and a guide to survival in the afterlife.

- Arranged in 190 chapters, the spells are in hieroglyphs on rolls of papyrus, each up to 98 ft (30 m) long.

- Copies of *The Book of the Dead* were placed in coffins with mummies. The magic contained in it was thought to

allow the dead to reach the kingdom of Osiris safely. Osiris was the supreme ruler and judge of the underworld.

- It was called *The Book of Coming-Forth-By-Day* by ancient Egyptians but was renamed *The Book of the Dead* by leading 19th-century Egyptologist Karl Lepsius.

- The finest copies had beautiful illustrations and were made by scribes of the New Kingdom (1550–1086 B.C.).

ANCIENT SCROLLS

- Many papyrus scrolls have been acquired by museums and collectors all over the world. Scrolls are named after their institution or owner.

- Many ancient scrolls contained literary or scientific works. Others were mundane lists, such as censuses, or letters of complaint.

- *The Salt Papyrus*, named after its owner and written in 1200 B.C., contains complaints from workmen about their foreman Paneb.

- Many papyri were devoted to medicine and cures. *The Brooklyn Papyrus* talks about treatments for snakebites.

- Stories and legends were popular subjects in the Middle Kingdom. *The Papyrus Westcar* relates *The Tale of Wonder*, a series of five stories, including that of a magician entertaining the king.

- Papyrus paper was used throughout the Greek and Roman eras and into the Islamic period, until it was replaced by cloth paper made of cotton rags.

- Cloth paper was introduced from the Far East in the 8th and 9th centuries A.D., and was cheaper and easier to produce.

- Egyptologists found more than 15,000 papyri at Oxyrhynchus in what was Upper Egypt between 1897 and 1922.

HOW PAPYRUS IS MADE

- Reeds of papyrus grew in the Nile Delta up to 20 ft (6 m) tall.
- The green outer layers of skin were peeled away (1), then cut into fine strips (2).

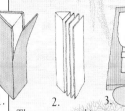

1.   2.   3.

Three steps to making papyrus

- The strips were first laid horizontally then vertically to make a square sheet (3).
- Linen was laid over the sheet and then pounded with a heavy stone or mallet to make the papyrus fibers stick together.
- When the sheets dried, they were joined together to form scrolls (*medjat*), usually with 20 squares to a scroll.
- Some scrolls were as long as 130 ft (40 m).
- When rolled up, the horizontal fibers were on the inside of the papyrus scroll.
- Writing and drawing were done on the inside of the scroll, and sometimes on the outside as well.
- Paper made from papyrus was long-lasting.

THE EGYPTIAN KITCHEN

MIDDLE-CLASS AND WEALTHY FAMILIES

- Kitchens in middle-class and wealthy homes were simple rooms at the back of the house, often in a courtyard that kept smells and smoke away from the rest of the house.

- Some kitchens had two sections: a cellar for storing food and fuel, and and another area for preparing food.

- Ovens were made of clay in the shape of a cylinder about 3 ft (1 m) high. They had a door at the bottom for ventilating the oven and removing ash.

- Fuel was put on a grill inside the oven. Wealthy families used charcoal and firewood for fuel.

- Cooking took place in a pot that rested on the hole at the top of the oven. The fire below heated the pot.

- The smoke from the oven was vented through one or two holes in the ceiling.

KITCHEN EQUIPMENT

- Larger kitchens had several tables. One was used to prepare meat and fish, another for vegetables. Trestle tables held joints of meat.

- There were many containers. Clay pots and pans were used for cooking; jugs for water, wine, and beer; and jars, trays, and baskets for serving food. Alabaster and other stone crockery was a luxury.

- Knives, choppers, and wooden utensils for stirring were kept on the tables ready for use.

- The storeroom held jars of wine, beer, oils, spices, and honey, and sacks of beans and lentils, grain, and other food.

Clay bowl decorated with hippopotamuses.

EATING TOGETHER

Families sat together on the floor to eat. Food was served in baskets, trays, or jars, and everyone helped themselves with their fingers. At parties, servants would pass food around on trays and in baskets. Although there were pottery cups for everyday use, individual plates were used only in wealthy households.

Servant carrying drinks on a tray.

WHO DID THE COOKING?

- In all but the wealthiest households, women and girls were expected to do all the food preparation and cooking – from grinding the flour to making the bread and beer.

- The women also made packed lunches for the men of the household to take to work and to school.

PEASANTS

- A peasant's kitchen was simple and sometimes smelly, with a roof made of branches or straw loosely woven to allow the smoke to escape.

- Ovens were very basic, usually a pot resting on three stones. Cheap fuel was burned underneath the pot.

- Peasants could not afford charcoal or firewood. Instead they burned dried animal dung or straw left over after the crops had been harvested.

- Flat pancakes or bread were baked on a heated stone.

- Peasants lived on a diet of bread, beer, and a few vegetables. Sometimes they ate rabbits, wild birds, and fish.

CRIME AND PUNISHMENT

CRIMINAL OFFENSES

Egyptian law was based on a commonsense view of right and wrong. Crimes included the following, with the least serious shown first:

- Fighting and drunkenness
- Petty theft and burglary
- Corruption by priests and officials
- Stealing from temples and tombs
- Avoiding military service
- Nonpayment of taxes
- Murder
- Conspiring to murder the king

THE JUDGES

- The pharaoh was the supreme judge in Egypt, but he rarely attended cases. He was represented by his viziers who acted for him in legal matters.

- Beneath the viziers were magistrates. They sat in judgment in the main law courts in Thebes.

- Outside the cities, local councils of elders in each town tried minor cases, such as the nonpayment of loans, and imposed penalties.

- Ancient Egyptians also consulted images of gods in temples for answers to their legal problems.

THE POLICE

By the New Kingdom (1550–1086 B.C.) there were three types of law enforcers – urban police made up of Nubian mercenaries (*medjays*); desert police (*nww*), who controlled raiding Bedouins; and border police. The police caught and punished criminals, guarded temples and tombs, and arrested those who hadn't paid their taxes.

An Egyptian policeman with his spear, sword, and shield.

TOMB RAIDERS

- Tomb raiding was a common practice in ancient Egypt.

- Hieroglyphic inscriptions in tombs warned tomb raiders against stealing the treasures. However, this was not enough to protect the tombs.

- Corrupt officials, police, and workmen at burial sites took bribes. Priests were also known to steal from their temples.

- Tomb raiders removed all the precious metals and jewels and abandoned the mummies.

- One gang of eight operating in Thebes in 1116 B.C. stole 32 lb (14.5 kg) of gold each. Eventually, three of the gang were caught, tried, and executed.

- No tomb was left untouched. Even Tutankhamun's showed some evidence of theft.

Amenhotep II's mummy, shown here in its sarcophagus, was stripped of its bandages by robbers looking for valuable amulets.

PUNISHMENT TO FIT THE CRIME

- Everyone in ancient Egypt received the same punishment for a crime regardless of his or her status.

- Thieves were fined and beaten.

- Running away from military service was punished by exile to the desert. Prisoners died of thirst if they tried to escape.

- Corrupt judges and officials could have their ears and noses cut off.

- Stealing from tombs was one of the worst crimes and resulted in the death penalty, by either being burned alive or being impaled on sharp stakes and left to die slowly and painfully.

- Instead of prisons there were labor camps where prisoners dug canals or dragged stones to building sites.

- One of the worst punishments was to work in the Nubian gold mines in the intense heat of the day.

ECONOMY AND TRADE

TRADE AND BARTER

Egyptian trade was based on a complicated system of exchange, called barter, which was used by the whole society.

- People were paid in oil, grain, or linen, which they could then exchange for other goods.

- Farmers often bartered some of their produce, such as wheat, barley, or livestock.

- An Egyptian might exchange a pair of sandals for a finely crafted walking stick, or a linen garment for a large quantity of food.

- Trading took place in town and village marketplaces.

- Even taxes were paid using the barter system, through work or produce. This may be how the pyramids were built, with citizens who owed taxes paying them off through labor.

- Traveling by land was time-consuming, so goods were often transported by boat. Traders sailed up and down the Nile and across the Mediterranean.

WEIGHTS AND MEASURES

- There were no coins until the 30th Dynasty (380–343 B.C.). Instead, prices were calculated against a scale of value based on weights of metal or stone. These were very precise and were checked regularly by temple and government officials.

Large balance for weighing produce

- The *shat*, *kite*, and *deben* were the weights that were used to establish the value of many goods.

- In later years, copper came to be used for small transactions, while silver and gold were used for things of higher value.

TRADING PARTNERS

Egypt was very wealthy and exchanged gold and surplus food in return for luxury goods from other countries.

- Incense, ebony, ivory, ostrich eggs, feathers, furs, and exotic animals came from Nubia and Punt.

- Silver came from Syria, and copper from Cyprus.

- Olive oil was obtained from Crete.

- Cedar wood came from Lebanon.

- Incense and spices came from Arabia.

- Lapis lazuli, a precious blue stone, came from Afghanistan.

TRADING CENTERS

- Because so many Greeks were interested in trading with Egypt, Naukratis in the Nile Delta became a Greek town.

- Alexandria, founded by Alexander the Great, became the capital and main port during the reign of Ptolemy I (305–282 B.C.).

- Alexandria was the most important trading center for Egypt, welcoming ships and traders from countries all over the Mediterranean.

- Many exotic goods from central Africa arrived through Aswan.

THE FIRST COINS IN EGYPT

Coins were first introduced in Egypt as currency during the 30th Dynasty (380–343 B.C.). The first coins minted bear the name of the ruler Teos (362–360 B.C.). The end of the barter system in ancient Egypt made it easier to trade with countries already using coins. Coins captured as war prizes from other nations were melted down into ingots (pieces of metal), which were also used as a form of currency.

Early Egyptian coins

EARLY PREDYNASTIC BOATS

- Simple boats used for fishing and hunting in the Delta were made of papyrus reeds lashed together.

- Some boats had upturned fronts, and poles that were used for steering.

OLD KINGDOM

- The first large boats made of wood appeared during this period (2686–2160 B.C.) and had steering oars, a mast, and a long narrow sail.

- They were used to carry blocks of stone to building sites.

- The remains of a boat from the Old Kingdom were found buried near the Great Pyramid at Giza in 1954.

MIDDLE KINGDOM

- Boats of this period (2040–1750 B.C.) looked very similar to earlier ones.

- Small improvements were made to oars (flatter), masts (collapsible), and cabins (placed at the back of the boat).

THE IMPORTANCE OF SHIPS

Boats and ships were an essential part of everyday life in Egypt.

- Vessels were used for a variety of purposes, including traveling, fighting, fishing, trading, and religious ceremonies.

- Every town along the Nile had a riverside dock and many temples and palaces had private docks.

Gods and kings were thought to travel to the underworld in boats.

- Funerary barques (model boats) were placed in pharaohs' tombs, ready for the pharaoh's journey through the afterlife.

148

NEW KINGDOM

- During this period (1550–1086 B.C.), many specialized boats appeared.

- Ships' cabins could be built onto the front, back, and middle of the vessel, and the sail was wider than it was high.

- Some boats were manned by as many as 15 oarsmen and one helmsman.

- Some large vessels could carry up to 300 tons (295 tonnes) of cargo on deck.

LATE AND GREEK PERIOD

- The Greek and Phoenician influence on ship-building in Egypt was at its height during this period (661–332 B.C.). This is seen in the long, low hulls and the lion figureheads at the end of the prows.

- Nekau II (610–595 B.C.) created the first full Egyptian navy. It was manned by Greek mercenaries.

- During the Battle of Actium (31 B.C.), the ships of the Roman general Octavian (63 B.C.–A.D. 14) defeated the Egyptian navy of Cleopatra VII (51–30 B.C.).

EGYPTIAN ARMY DEFEATS THE SEA PEOPLES

During the eighth year of the reign of Ramses III (1184–1153 B.C.), a mixed group of Mediterranean people, the Sea Peoples, attacked Egypt from the land and the sea with the intention of settling there. Ramses III's army in Syria-Palestine defeated the land attack, and his army in the Delta destroyed the Sea Peoples' fleet. To celebrate the victory, Ramses had scenes from the battle at the Delta recreated in reliefs on the walls at Medinet Habu, a large royal temple south of Thebes.

A relief on the walls of Medinet Habu showing Ramses's defeat of the Sea Peoples.

IMPORTANT CITIES

MEMPHIS, THE FIRST CAPITAL CITY

- Said to be founded by the 1st-dynasty ruler Menes in 3100 B.C., Memphis was the capital and main port of Egypt until the 4th century B.C.

- The creator-god Ptah and his wife Sekhmet were the deities of Memphis. Ptah's temple was the most important building in the city.

- The Colossus of Ramses II and his temple were built here.

- Pharaohs built most of their palaces, temples, pyramids, and tombs at nearby Giza and Saqqara.

SAQQARA

- Part of the royal cemetery of Memphis, Saqqara was used as a burial site from 3100 B.C. until A.D. 540.

- As well as the famous Step Pyramid, Saqqara has many mastaba (tombs), temples, and other pyramids. There are also underground galleries and shafts that have been used by robbers through the ages.

- Many of the interiors of the pyramids are covered in hieroglyphic inscriptions known as the *Pyramid Texts*. These are short spells to help the dead ruler on his journey to the afterlife.

GIZA

Giza was part of the royal cemetery at Memphis. Many rulers from the Old Kingdom (2686–2181 B.C.) built pyramids here, including Khufu (2587–2564 B.C.), Khafra (2556–2530 B.C.), and Menkaura (2526–2506 B.C.). Khufu's Great Pyramid took nearly 20 years to complete. It is thought to have required a work force of 30,000 men.

Khafra's pyramid at Giza was guarded by the Sphinx, who had the head of the pharaoh and the body of a lion.

THEBES, CHIEF CITY OF UPPER EGYPT

- Thebes is the Greek name for the ancient town of Waset. It was the official capital of the New Kingdom (c.1550–1086 B.C.), and an important religious center.

- Thebes was well situated between the Delta and the African provinces. Caravans from Nubia carrying gold, ebony, ivory, ostrich feathers, and gum passed through Thebes. As a result, trade flourished here.

- The Great Temple of Amun-Ra was begun in the Middle Kingdom (2040–1750 B.C.) and built over 2,000 years. It was mainly dedicated to the gods Amun-Ra, Mut, and Montu.

- Many monuments were built under Amenhotep III (c.1390–1352 B.C.) and Ramses II (c.1279–1213 B.C.).

- Ramses II also built the Great Hypostyle Hall (columned hall), measuring 340 ft (102 m) long, 175 ft (53 m) wide, with 134 columns 85 ft (25 m) high to support the ceiling.

- Thebes ruled Egypt for more than 500 years before being invaded by the Assyrians in the seventh century B.C. The two great temples of Karnak and Luxor are all that remain today.

HELIOPOLIS

- The city of On, called Heliopolis (City of the Sun) by the Greeks, was one of the oldest and most important cult centers in ancient Egypt.

- The first sun temple dedicated to Ra was built there in 2600 B.C.

- Now buried under Cairo, some of its monuments have been transported to other places.

- Cleopatra's Needle, an obelisk from Thutmose III's reign (1479–1425 B.C.), was brought to London in 1878.

ALEXANDRIA, CITY OF THE PTOLEMIES

- Alexander the Great founded this city in 331 B.C. on the site of an earlier town called Raqote.

- It became the capital city of Egypt during the Greek (Ptolemaic) period (332–30 B.C.) and was a major center for trade and learning.

- It was famous for The Great Library of Alexandria, which housed more than 700,000 books, and for the Pharos Lighthouse and many other important monuments and temples.

- By the 1st century B.C., half a million people lived in the city.

TEMPLES

HOUSES OF THE GODS

- Each temple in ancient Egypt was dedicated to the worship of a particular god.

- Early temples were made of reeds and mud bricks. Later temples used longer-lasting and richly decorated stone to preserve the houses of the gods and their priestly rituals.

- Few temples survive from the Old and Middle Kingdoms (2686–2160 B.C. and 2040–1750 B.C.). They were looted and built over.

- The Temple of Amun at Karnak is the most elaborate, and the Temple of Horus at Edfu the best preserved.

TEMPLE COMPLEXES

- The priesthood in ancient Egypt was rich and powerful. Temples had vast tracts of agricultural land with farm laborers who worked it.

- Temple complexes were like small towns, with houses and offices for priests and scribes, and storage areas for agricultural produce.

- Temples also ran schools for scribes, and many had libraries, law courts, and tax and administrative offices.

- Craftsmen making furniture, pottery, paper, leather goods, textiles, and jewelry had workshops within the temple complex.

HOW WERE THEY STRUCTURED?

- All temples were based on a similar structure. They were enclosed by a wall that surrounded a courtyard and a sanctuary – a small, dark room where offerings to the gods were made. Additions in the New Kingdom (1550–1086 B.C.) included pylons (gateways) and hypostyle halls with massive columns.

- A statue of the temple's god was placed in the sanctuary and was

thought to contain the spirit of that particular god.

- Priests' rituals involved purifying the sanctuary and offering the gods food, clothing, and cosmetics.

- Ordinary people prayed in the courtyard or outside the walls of the enclosure.

- Many temples were highly decorated, and the walls were brightly painted.

GREAT TEMPLES AND THEIR REMAINS

KARNAK

- The temple complex at Karnak was the largest in Egypt. It contained a huge number of buildings. The first temple was built by Senusret I (1965–1920 B.C.), and other temples and buildings were added later.

Royal statues in the temple complex at Karnak

- The largest temples were dedicated to Amun, the state god, Mut, the vulture goddess, and Montu, a local war god.

- Karnak's priests employed thousands of people.

- By Roman times, Karnak covered 1.9 sq miles (3 sq km) with shrines, halls, pylons, statues, and obelisks.

THE WEST BANK – THE RAMESSEUM AND MEDINET HABU

- The West Bank at Thebes contains many palaces, temples, and tombs, which are all interconnected.

- Ramses II (1279–1213 B.C.) built one of Egypt's most impressive mortuary temples (where the body was embalmed). It is called the Ramesseum and is almost as large as St. Peter's Basilica in Rome, Italy.

Statues of Ramses II in the Ramesseum

- The remains of a royal palace, granaries, storerooms, and a school for scribes have also been found in the Ramesseum.

- The traveler Diodorus Siculus (1st century B.C.) mistakenly called the Ramesseum the "tomb of Ozymandias." The English poet Percy Bysshe Shelley (1792–1822) was also inspired to write about it in *Ozymandias of Egypt*.

- The mortuary temple of Ramses III (1184–1153 B.C.) at Medinet Habu was modeled after the Ramesseum. It was built to celebrate Ramses III's achievements – including his defeat of the Sea Peoples and the Libyans.

Colonnade at Medinet Habu

THE PYRAMIDS

FUNCTION, SHAPE, AND SIZE

- Pyramids were funerary monuments, eternal resting places from which the pharaohs protected their kingdoms and subjects in the afterlife.

- The triangular shape gave the impression that the pyramids received the rays of the divine sun.

- Believed to be staircases to heaven, the pyramids reunited the pharaohs with Ra, the sun god and ruler of the heavenly kingdom.

- The average stone block in a pyramid weighs 2.5 tons (2.54 tonnes), and the largest stone slabs weigh 49 tons (50 tonnes).

HEIGHT

Just how tall the pyramids are can be seen in the comparisons below.

Pyramid of Khufu 482 ft (147 m)
Pyramid of Khafra 472 ft (144 m)
Pyramid of Menkaura 218 ft (68 m)

Modern-day comparisons
St. Paul's Cathedral 360 ft (110 m)
Statue of Liberty 300 ft (92 m)
Arc de Triomphe 165 ft (49.5 m)

PYRAMIDS WORLDWIDE

- The Mayas and Aztecs of Mexico and Central America built flat-topped towers in steep receding blocks and often used them as temples. Mayan pyramids in Mexico were crowned with ritual chambers.

Aztec temples in Mexico

- The Romans also built pyramidal tombs. The most famous example was the Pyramid of Cestius (62–12 B.C.), a high-ranking official in Rome. The pyramid was built with cement, covered with marble, and had an interior tomb vault 116 ft (35 m) high.

- The Chinese architect I.M. Pei added a large glass pyramid to the entrance of the Louvre Museum in Paris, France, in 1989. Stainless-steel tubes form the 69 ft (21 m) high frame.

THE FIRST PYRAMID

The Step Pyramid at Saqqara was the first step pyramid ever built. Thought to be designed for King Djoser by the great architect Imhotep around 2680 B.C., it rose to a height of 198 ft (60 m). The pyramid is a series of six mastabas (tombs) built one on top of another. The base is 398 ft (121 m) long and 358 ft (109 m) wide.

The pyramid complex is surrounded by an outer wall, 5,397 ft (1,645 m) wide and 34 ft (10.5 m) high. Its white limestone façade was designed to imitate other palace façades. The wall had 14 entrances, but only one was real.

The Step Pyramid was built entirely of stone.

GRAVE ROBBERS

- After 4,000 years of looting, not one Egyptian pyramid has survived intact.

- Threatening inscriptions carved on the walls of burial chambers warned grave robbers against stealing furnishings and offerings. Some described an evil serpent that would blind or poison the intruder.

- Builders tried to fool thieves by building passageways, then sealing them with stones.

- In the New Kingdom (1550–1086 B.C.), tombs were cut into valley rockfaces to hide them from grave robbers.

- Papyrus records of grave robber trials contain detailed descriptions of how the gangs operated, which tombs they robbed, and how much they stole.

- Even some Egyptian kings stole from the tombs of their ancestors. Amenemhat I (1985–1955 B.C.), the founder of the 12th Dynasty, used stone from the 4th-dynasty temples of Cheops (Khufu, 2587–2564 B.C.). The crime was easily detected because the stones from Cheops' temples were marked with his name.

CREATION MYTHS

IN THE BEGINNING

- The ancient Egyptians had many creation myths. In fact, every major temple had its own version.

- They thought that a number of their gods were responsible for creating the world, including Amun-Ra, Aten, Atum, Khnum, Neith, Ptah, Ra, Sobek, and Thoth.

- Three basic myths emerged. All agreed that before the beginning of the world there was a dark watery chaos, ruled by the god Nun.

THE MYTH FROM MEMPHIS

- This creation myth dates from the New Kingdom (1550–1086 B.C.) and tells how the creator god Ptah shaped the world like a master craftsman.

- Ptah created all the gods, people, and animals by his thoughts and words. They emerged when he pronounced their names.

- This story is recorded in hieroglyphs on a 25th-dynasty slab of volcanic rock found in Memphis.

THE MYTH OF THE ENNEAD FROM HELIOPOLIS

- Arising from the temple of the sun god at Heliopolis, this creation myth dates from at least the Old Kingdom (2686–2160 B.C.).

- The sun god Atum was said to have created himself out of Nun's watery depths, through some form of magic.

- By spitting and sneezing, Atum produced new life and split it into two elements: air (the god Shu) and moisture (the goddess Tefnut).

- Shu and Tefnut gave birth to Nut, the goddess of heaven, and Geb, the god of earth. They were in love and had two sons, Osiris and Seth, and two daughters, Isis and Nephthys. In some versions, Horus is their fifth child.

- The linking of heaven and earth in Nut and Geb became the model for kingship – the king was considered to be a living god on earth.

- According to legend, Osiris was the first pharaoh of Egypt, and together with Isis, his sister-wife, he ruled over a peaceful and prosperous kingdom.

- Together these gods shaped and created the world, and afterward protected it, ensuring that good prevailed over evil.

THE MYTH FROM HERMOPOLIS MAGNA

- Dating from the Middle Kingdom (2040–1750 B.C.), a well-known creation myth from Hermopolis describes how four pairs of gods called the Ogdoad (*khmun*) emerged to shape the universe.

- The Ogdoad symbolized different aspects of the chaos before creation.

- They appeared as frog gods and snake goddesses. Each frog god was paired off with a snake goddess.

- These four pairs created the "primeval hill," the main symbol of creation. On it they placed the egg of the sun god, from which the creator, Atum or Thoth, was born.

- Another creation myth from Hermopolis described a lotus flower that opened its petals, chasing away the darkness. The light of the sun was then able to shine on the earth for the first time.

The cartouche of Rameses II, which included the name of the sun god Ra.

CREATION VERSUS CHAOS

The sun god Ra traveled across the sky daily, dispensing heat and light.

All myths seem to agree that, when life was created, destructive forces came into being at the same time. These took the form of chaos monsters such as Apophis, who tried to destroy the work of the creator. Every night and at the change of each season, the forces of creation battled against the forces of chaos to keep the world safe. The sun god Ra's appearance at sunrise, his journey across the sky, and his disappearance below the horizon every evening represented this constant struggle.

THE FIVE ELEMENTS OF THE PERSONALITY

- Ancient Egyptians believed that a person's body housed the personality. It was made up of five essential elements – the *Akh*, the *Ba*, the *Ka*, the Name, and the Shadow.

- When a person died, the five elements were released and separated. However, they still remained closely linked to the body.

- For the elements to live on in the afterlife, a physical representation of the body was needed. The body was replaced by a statue or other image of the dead person, or by a mummy.

Guardian statues, such as this one found in Tutankhamun's tomb, protected the mummy and allowed the elements to survive in the afterlife.

THE BODY

The Egyptians believed that the five elements of the personality left the body at death, but were reunited once the body was buried. The process of mummification was therefore very important. Preserving the body provided a home for the elements in the afterlife and ensured eternal life for the deceased.

THE NAME

- This element was vital to the identity of a person, and had to be given at birth. Names were chosen by what was in fashion at the time.

- The Name was a powerful part of the personality. After death, as long as the name was still spoken or written, the person's spirit continued to live.

- The removal of people's names from monuments was thought to harm their spirits in the afterlife because it destroyed their memory and existence.

THE BA

- This element was sometimes represented as a bird with a human head and arms.

- The *Ba* was released from the body on death and kept the same qualities it had when it lived in the body.

- After death, the job of the *Ba* was to journey from the tomb to rejoin the *Ka*, so that the person could be transformed into an *Akh*.

- The *Ba* moved freely between heaven and earth, journeying to and from the land of the living.

- It was closely linked to the physical body and needed food.

THE KA

- This element of the personality was represented as a pair of outstretched arms that warded off evil. It was the life force of the individual.

- The *Ka* came into being when a person was born, but had its own personality and led an independent existence during that person's life.

- After death, the *Ka* lived on. Like the *Ba*, it needed food in order to fulfill its role. Offerings of food and drink were left in tombs to feed it.

- When the *Ba* and the *Ka* were reunited after death, they transformed the person into an *Akh*.

THE AKH

- This element was represented as a crested ibis, a type of bird that helped the dead reach the stars on their journey to the afterlife.

- The *Akh*, a "transfigured being," achieved an ideal state after death if the deceased had a good burial, and if provisions were made for the *Ba*, *Ka*, Name, and Shadow.

- The *Akh* also represented spirits and demons, which acted as mediums between humans and the gods.

THE SHADOW

- This element (*shwt*) was represented as a feather, or palm fan. It helped protect a person from harm in life and in death.

- The Shadow was powerful and able to move at great speeds. It was black, had the same outline and appearance as the living person, and could not be separated from its owner.

- It was associated with restfulness, well-being, good health, happiness, and long life.

ANCIENT TOURISTS

EARLY VISITORS

We know a great deal about Egypt from the writings of ancient travelers and historians.

• The Greeks traded extensively with Egypt from about 700 B.C. Many Greeks visited and lived in Egypt. They left records of their travels in papyrus scrolls and books.

• The Greek writer Plutarch (c.A.D. 46–126), author of *Parallel Lives of Famous Greeks and Romans*, traveled widely in Egypt. He wrote about Horus, Seth, and Osiris.

• According to legend, Menelaus the Greek king visited Egypt on his way back to Greece with Helen of Troy.

HERODOTUS – THE FIRST TRAVEL WRITER

• The Greek traveler and historian Herodotus (c.484–420 B.C.), wrote nine books of *Histories*, including one on Egypt.

• He traveled through Egypt in about 450 B.C., and talked to priests about the pyramids, festivals, and mummification. His description of the method of embalming bodies is one of the most detailed of this time.

• He visited the pyramid complex of Amenemhat III (1854–1808 B.C.) at Hawara and described its 3,000 rooms connected by winding passages. Many of the monuments he wrote about have since disappeared, but his works have helped archaeologists relocate a number of sites.

• His descriptions of Hawara made it a top tourist spot for Greek and Roman travelers of the time. Hawara was first identified by the German Egyptologist Karl Lepsius in 1843, and the English archaeologist Flinders Petrie excavated there in 1888 and 1911.

• Herodotus was a keen observer of customs and wrote about almost every aspect of Egyptian life.

• He recorded that priests shaved their heads and had no body hair, that they washed twice a day and twice at night in cold water, and that even though they could marry, they were only allowed to have only one wife and were not allowed to have children while they were in office as priests.

STRABO – THE ANCIENT GEOGRAPHER

- The Greek historian and geographer Strabo (c. 63 B.C.–A.D. 21) was also a famous cartographer and made surprisingly accurate maps of the known world around the Mediterranean Sea.

- He spent several years in Alexandria and wrote about Egypt in his eighth book of *Geography*.

- Strabo visited Lower Egypt and the Theban monuments, including the Colossi of Memnon, which he noted made a whistling sound.

- He visited the First Cataract on the Nile in about 25 B.C. and saw the Nilometer at Elephantine.

- He also visited the Serapeum at Saqqara. Centuries later, Auguste Mariette (1821–1881), a French Egyptologist, dug it up using Strabo's account as a guide.

DIODORUS SICULUS

- The Sicilian-born historian Diodorus Siculus (c.90–21 B.C.) traveled extensively through Egypt, gathering material for Book I of his *Bibliotheca Historica*.

- He provided a valuable insight into the geography, history, and customs of ancient Egypt, including the processes and rituals of mummification.

- He was a keen food critic and enjoyed Egyptian beer – he said it was almost as good as wine.

- He also observed, perhaps not accurately, that in times of famine Egyptians preferred to eat each other than their sacred animals.

Sphinx with the face of Ramses II, who built the famous Ramesseum, visited by Siculus.

- Siculus is also responsible for incorrectly labeling Ramses II's tomb as the "tomb of Ozymandias."

CLEOPATRA

THE LAST QUEEN OF EGYPT

One of the most fascinating figures in history, Cleopatra has inspired many artists, sculptors, and writers in the 2,000 years since her death.

- Cleopatra VII Philopator (51–30 B.C.) was descended from Alexander the Great and was the last ruler of the Ptolemaic dynasty.

- She became queen at the age of 17, and ruled Egypt during one of the most chaotic periods in the country's long history.

- She broke with centuries of Ptolemaic tradition by learning to speak Egyptian and worshipping the traditional gods.

- Historical sources such as Plutarch describe Cleopatra as extremely intelligent, well educated, and cultured. As well as having an interest in the sciences, she spoke Egyptian, Greek, Arabic, and Hebrew.

- She is famous for her relationships with two of the most powerful men of her day, Julius Caesar (100–44 B.C.) and Mark Antony (c.83–30 B.C.)

CLEOPATRA'S CARPET TRICK

To gain access to Caesar, Cleopatra had herself rolled up in a carpet and carried into his presence. According to the Greek writer Plutarch (c.A.D. 46–120) in his *Life of Caesar*, the Roman leader "was captivated by her conversation and grace." She became his mistress and secured the Egyptian throne for herself.

A relief showing Cleopatra and Caesarion, her son by Caesar, making an offering to Hathor.

TUMULTUOUS TIMES

- Cleopatra came to the throne at a time of civil war and unrest. Egypt was torn apart by famine, rebellion, and an unstable economy.

- Forced to flee Alexandria by her scheming brother-husband, Ptolemy XIII, Cleopatra set about regaining power on her own.

- Rome, also torn apart by warring factions, saw this as an opportunity to make Egypt a part of its empire. Rome needed Egypt's gold and wheat.

- Caesar's rise to power in Rome meant that Egypt and Cleopatra's fates were now in his hands. *Julius Caesar*

- After meeting Cleopatra, Caesar confirmed her as queen of Egypt. She had maintained her country's independence, and ruled with Caesar's support.

- Caesar's assassination in 44 B.C. threw Rome back into political turmoil. Caesar's heir, Octavian (63 B.C.–A.D. 14), fought Mark Antony for the control of Rome and Egypt.

- Mark Antony set sail for Alexandria. On meeting Cleopatra, he too fell in love, and confirmed her as queen of Egypt. Together they dreamed of ruling an empire.

THE END OF PHARAONIC EGYPT

- Octavian's decisive victory over Antony and Cleopatra at the Battle of Actium in 31 B.C. gave him sole control over the Mediterranean and the Roman world.

- Cleopatra and Mark Antony managed to escape unhurt to Alexandria. However, as Octavian approached Alexandria, Mark Antony committed suicide by falling on his sword.

- Cleopatra, on learning of Mark Antony's death, and unable to tolerate her country being ruled by Rome, also committed suicide. Legend has it that she was bitten by an asp (cobra), which was hidden in a basket of figs.

- Cleopatra's death marked the end of pharaonic Egypt and heralded its inclusion into the Roman empire.

FAMOUS EGYPTOLOGISTS & THEIR DISCOVERIES

JEAN-FRANÇOIS CHAMPOLLION

- This French Egyptologist (1790–1832) deciphered the hieroglyphic inscriptions on the Rosetta Stone in 1822. This meant that Egyptian texts could be understood for the first time. The Rosetta Stone is now in the British Museum, London.

- He excavated at Karnak in 1828, moved on to Nubia in 1829, then returned to Luxor where he read, translated, and recorded a wide range of hieroglyphic texts.

- He bought more than 100 works for the Louvre Museum, in Paris.

KARL RICHARD LEPSIUS

- This German archaeologist (1810–1884) was considered to be one of the fathers of Egyptology. He was particularly interested in funerary papyri, and coined the term *The Book of the Dead* for the scrolls placed in coffins to protect the dead.

- He discovered the *Canopus Decree*, a document that helped to decipher demotic (everyday) script.

AUGUSTE MARIETTE

- In 1851, this French Egyptologist (1821–1881) found the famous Serapeum, the huge burial site of the sacred Apis bulls at Saqqara. The Apis bull represented the god Ptah.

- He also found 134 sphinxes and an underground passageway with 28 chambers, including an intact burial chamber from the reign of Ramses II (1279–1213 B.C.).

CHRISTIANE DESROCHES-NOBLECOURT

- This French Egyptologist (born 1913) was in charge of the Egyptian collection of the Louvre Museum, in Paris, during World War II. She organized the relocation of the treasures to protect them from bombing.

- She was appointed by the international organization UNESCO to save the temples of Nubia that were threatened by the construction of the Aswan Dam.

- Her international appeal for help resulted in 14 of the most important temples being moved to avoid being flooded by Lake Nasser.

HOWARD CARTER

This English archaeologist (1874–1939) discovered the tomb of Tutankhamun in 1922, significant because the tomb had not been spoiled by grave robbers. When 17 people associated with the discovery died unexpectedly within a few years, there was speculation that a curse had guarded the tomb.

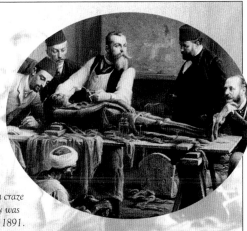

During Carter's lifetime, there was a craze for all things Egyptian. This mummy was unwrapped at the Cairo Museum in 1891.

EMILE BRUGSCH

- In 1881, this German archaeologist (1842–1930) found the sarcophagi and mummies of the greatest pharaohs of the New Kingdom (1550–1086 B.C.) at Deir el-Bahri. These included Ahmose I, Amenhotep I, Thutmose I and III, Ramses I, II, III, IX, Sety I, Hatshepsut, and Nefertari.

- The mummies were put there by priests in about 1000 B.C. to keep them safe from grave robbers, who, after looting the tombs, had discarded them.

- They remained undiscovered until Brugsch found them, with the help of a former grave robber, Mohammed Abd-el Rassul.

FLINDERS PETRIE

- This English archaeologist (1853–1942) discovered over 3,000 tombs from the Predynastic era (5500–3100 B.C.) at Naqada, 10 miles (16 km) north of Thebes, in 1894.

- This was the first Predynastic discovery and provided evidence for the origins of pharaonic culture.

- By studying the pottery pieces he had excavated, he developed his "Sequence Dating" theory, which dated pottery by the progression of its style. It enabled him to create a chronology of the Predynastic era, even though there were no ancient texts from this period.

REFERENCE SECTION

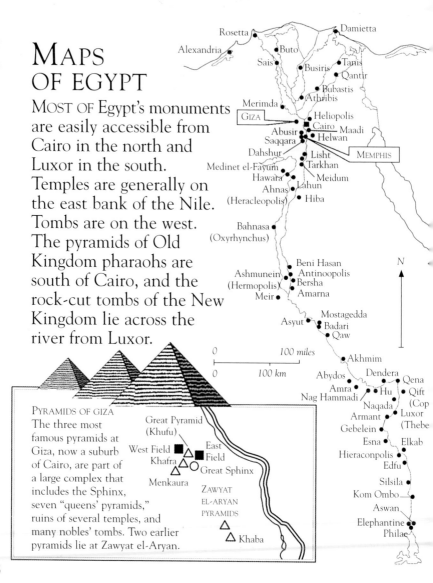

Maps
of Egypt

Most of Egypt's monuments are easily accessible from Cairo in the north and Luxor in the south. Temples are generally on the east bank of the Nile. Tombs are on the west. The pyramids of Old Kingdom pharaohs are south of Cairo, and the rock-cut tombs of the New Kingdom lie across the river from Luxor.

Pyramids of Giza
The three most famous pyramids at Giza, now a suburb of Cairo, are part of a large complex that includes the Sphinx, seven "queens' pyramids," ruins of several temples, and many nobles' tombs. Two earlier pyramids lie at Zawyat el-Aryan.

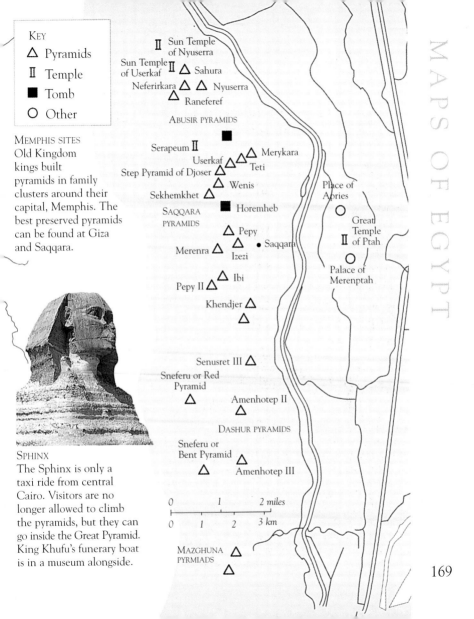

KEY
△ Pyramids
Ⅱ Temple
■ Tomb
○ Other

MEMPHIS SITES
Old Kingdom kings built pyramids in family clusters around their capital, Memphis. The best preserved pyramids can be found at Giza and Saqqara.

Ⅱ Sun Temple of Nyuserra

Sun Temple of Userkaf Ⅱ △ Sahura

Neferirkara △ △ Nyuserra

△ Raneferef

ABUSIR PYRAMIDS

■

Serapeum Ⅱ

Userkaf △△△ Merykara
Teti

Step Pyramid of Djoser △

△ Wenis

Sekhemkhet △

Place of Apries ○

■ Horemheb

SAQQARA PYRAMIDS

△ Pepy

Great Temple Ⅱ of Ptah

Merenra △ △ • Saqqara
Izezi

○ Palace of Merenptah

Pepy II △ △ Ibi

Khendjer △

△

Senusret III △

Sneferu or Red Pyramid
△

△ Amenhotep II

DASHUR PYRAMIDS

Sneferu or Bent Pyramid
△

△ Amenhotep III

SPHINX
The Sphinx is only a taxi ride from central Cairo. Visitors are no longer allowed to climb the pyramids, but they can go inside the Great Pyramid. King Khufu's funerary boat is in a museum alongside.

0   1   2 miles

0   1   2   3 km

MAZGHUNA PYRMIADS △

△

169

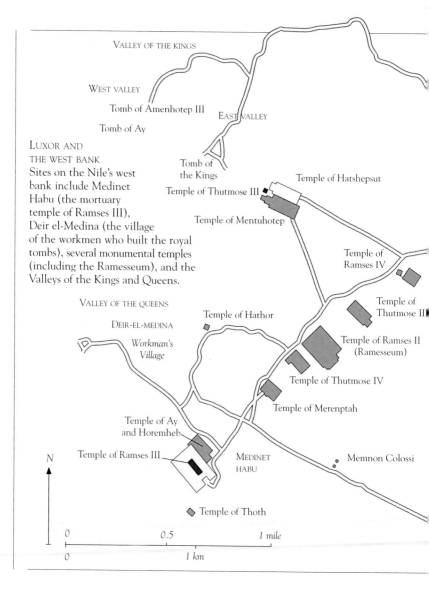

VALLEY OF THE KINGS

WEST VALLEY

Tomb of Amenhotep III

EAST VALLEY

Tomb of Ay

LUXOR AND
THE WEST BANK
Sites on the Nile's west
bank include Medinet
Habu (the mortuary
temple of Ramses III),
Deir el-Medina (the village
of the workmen who built the royal
tombs), several monumental temples
(including the Ramesseum), and the
Valleys of the Kings and Queens.

Tomb of
the Kings

Temple of Thutmose III

Temple of Hatshepsut

Temple of Mentuhotep

Temple of
Ramses IV

Temple of
Thutmose III

VALLEY OF THE QUEENS

DEIR-EL-MEDINA

Workman's
Village

Temple of Hathor

Temple of Ramses II
(Ramesseum)

Temple of Thutmose IV

Temple of Merenptah

Temple of Ay
and Horemheb

Temple of Ramses III

MEDINET
HABU

Memnon Colossi

N

◆ Temple of Thoth

| 0 | 0.5 | 1 mile |

| 0 | 1 km |

VALLEY OF THE KINGS
The many rock-cut tombs in this desolate valley include those of Tutankhamun (whose mummy has been returned to his burial chamber), Ramses VI (which has brightly painted walls), and Sety I (one of the deepest).

Temple of Sety I

COLOSSI OF MEMNON
A short ferry trip across the Nile from Luxor takes visitors to the West Bank. One of the first sights is nearly all that remains of Amenhotep III's mortuary temple – the massive Colossi of Memnon.

THE WEST BANK SITES

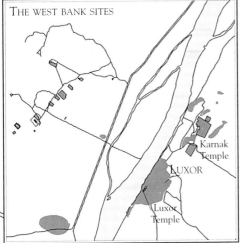

Karnak Temple

LUXOR

Luxor Temple

LUXOR
This modern city lies near the site of Thebes, the New Kingdom capital. In ancient times, the great temples of Karnak and Luxor were linked by an avenue of ram-headed sphinxes. Luxor Museum has a fine collection of antiquities.

KINGDOMS AND DYNASTIES

THE PHARAOHS ruled Egypt for more than 3,000 years. Historians usually divide this vast stretch of time into 31 dynasties. All of the dates given in these tables are approximate.

DJOSER

EARLY DYNASTIC PERIOD
3100–2613 B.C.
FIRST DYNASTY
(3100–2690 B.C.)
Narmer
Aha
Djer
Djet
Den
Anedjib
Semerkhet
Qaa

SECOND DYNASTY
(2890–2686 B.C.)
Hotepsekhemwy
Nebra
Nynetjer
Peribsen
Khasekhem

OLD KINGDOM
2686–2160 B.C.
THIRD DYNASTY
(2686–2613 B.C.)
Sanakht
Djoser
Sekhemkhet
Khaba
Huni

FOURTH DYNASTY
(2613–2494 B.C.)
Sneferu
Khufu (Cheops)
Djedefra
Khafra (Chephren)
Menkaura (Mycerinus)
Shepseskaf

FIFTH DYNASTY
(2494–2345 B.C.)
Userkaf
Sahura
Neferirkara
Shepseskara
Neferefra
Nyuserra
Menkauhor
Djedkara
Unas

SIXTH DYNASTY
(2345–2181 B.C.)
Teti
Userkara
Pepy I
Merenra
Pepy II

SEVENTH/EIGHTH DYNASTIES
(2181–2125 B.C.)

FIRST INTERMEDIATE
PERIOD 2160–2040 B.C.
NINTH DYNASTY
(2160–2130 B.C.)
TENTH DYNASTY
(2125–2025 B.C.)
Meryibra Khety
Wahkara Khety
Merykara

ELEVENTH DYNASTY (THEBES)
(2125–1985 B.C.)
Mentuhotep I
Intef I
Intef II
Intef III

MIDDLE KINGDOM
2040–1750 B.C.
ELEVENTH DYNASTY (Continued)
Mentuhotep II   2055–2004 B.C.

TWELFTH DYNASTY
(1985–1795 B.C.)
Amenemhat I   1985–1955 B.C.
Senusret I   1965–1920 B.C.
Amenemhat II   1922–1878 B.C.
Senusret II   1880–1874 B.C.
Senusret III   1874–1855 B.C.
Amenemhat III   1854–1808 B.C.
Amenemhat IV   1808–1799 B.C.
Sobekkara Sobekneferu
                1799–1795 B.C.

SECOND INTERMEDIATE
PERIOD
1750–1650 B.C.
THIRTEENTH DYNASTY
(1795–1650 B.C.)
Sobekhotep III
Sobekhotep IV
Neferhotep I

FOURTEENTH DYNASTY
(1750–1650 B.C.)

FIFTEENTH DYNASTY
(1650–1550 B.C.)
Khyan
Apepi

SIXTEENTH DYNASTY
(1650–1550 B.C.)

SEVENTEENTH DYNASTY
(1650–1550 B.C.)
Intef V
Taa I
Kamose

NEW KINGDOM
1550–1086 B.C.
EIGHTEENTH DYNASTY
(1550–1295 B.C.)

Ahmose I	1550–1525 B.C.
Amenhotep I	1525–1504 B.C.
Thutmose I	1504–1492 B.C.
Thutmose II	1492–1479 B.C.
Hatshepsut	1479–1457 B.C.
Thutmose III	1479–1425 B.C.
Amenhotep II	1427–1400 B.C.
Thutmose IV	1400–1390 B.C.
Amenhotep III	1390–1352 B.C.
Amenhotep IV (Akhenaten)	1352–1336 B.C.
Tutankhamun	1336–1327 B.C.
Ay	1327–1323 B.C.
Horemheb	1323–1295 B.C.

NINETEENTH DYNASTY
(1295–1186 B.C.)

Ramses I	1295–1294 B.C.
Sety I	1294–1279 B.C.
Ramses II	1279–1213 B.C.
Merenptah	1213–1203 B.C.
Sety II	1200–1194 B.C.
Saptah	1194–1188 B.C.
Tausret	1188–1186 B.C.

TWENTIETH DYNASTY
(1186–1069 B.C.)

Setnakht	1186–1184 B.C.
Ramses III	1184–1153 B.C.
Ramses IV	1153–1147 B.C.
Ramses V	1147–1143 B.C.
Ramses VI	1143–1136 B.C.
Ramses VII	1136–1129 B.C.
Ramses VIII	1129–1126 B.C.
Ramses IX	1126–1108 B.C.
Ramses X	1108–1099 B.C.
Ramses XI	1099–1069 B.C.

THIRD INTERMEDIATE
PERIOD
1086–661 B.C.
TWENTY-FIRST DYNASTY
(1069–945 B.C.)

Smendes	1069–1043 B.C.
Psusennes I	1039–991 B.C.
Amenemope	993–984 B.C.
Saamun	978–959 B.C.
Psusennes II	959–945 B.C.

TWENTY-SECOND DYNASTY
(945–715 B.C.)

Sheshonq I	945–924 B.C.
Osorkon I	924–889 B.C.
Takelot I	889–874 B.C.
Osorkon II	874–850 B.C.
Takelot II	850–825 B.C.
Sheshonq III	825–773 B.C.
Pimay	773–767 B.C.
Sheshonq V	767–730 B.C.

TWENTY-THIRD DYNASTY
(818–715 B.C.)

Padibast I	818–793 B.C.
Osorkon III	777–749 B.C.

TWENTY-FOURTH DYNASTY
(727–715 B.C.)
Tefnakht

TWENTY-FIFTH DYNASTY
(NUBIAN KINGS)
(747–656 B.C.)

Piy	747–716 B.C.
Shabako	716–702 B.C.
Shabitko	702–690 B.C.
Taharqo	690–664 B.C.
Tanutamani	664–656 B.C.

LATE PERIOD
661–332 B.C.
TWENTY-SIXTH DYNASTY
(664–525 B.C.)

Psamtek I	664–610 B.C.
Nekau II	610–595 B.C.
Psamtek II	595–589 B.C.
Apries	589–570 B.C.
Amasis	570–526 B.C.
Psamtek III	526–525 B.C.

TWENTY-SEVENTH DYNASTY
(PERSIAN KINGS)
(525–404 B.C.)

Cambyses	525–522 B.C.
Darius I	522–486 B.C.
Xerxes	486–465 B.C.
Artaxerxes I	465–424 B.C.
Darius II	424–405 B.C.
Artaxerxes II	405–359 B.C.

TWENTY-EIGHTH DYNASTY
(404–399 B.C.)

Amyrtaeus	404–399 B.C.

TWENTY-NINTH DYNASTY
(399–380 B.C.)

Nepherites I	399–393 B.C.
Achoris	392–380 B.C.

THIRTIETH DYNASTY
(380–343 B.C.)

Nectanebo I	380–362 B.C.
Teos	362–360 B.C.
Nectanebo II	360–343 B.C.

THIRTY-FIRST DYNASTY
(PERSIAN KINGS)
(343–332 B.C.)

Artaxerxes III	343–338 B.C.
Arses	338–336 B.C.
Darius III	336–332 B.C.

GREEK PERIOD
332–30 B.C.

Alexander the Great	332–323 B.C.
Philip Arrhidaeus	323–317 B.C.
Alexander IV	317–305 B.C.
Ptolemy I	305–282 B.C.
Ptolemy II	284–246 B.C.
Ptolemy III	246–222 B.C.
Ptolemy IV	222–205 B.C.
Ptolemy V	205–180 B.C.
Ptolemy VI	180–145 B.C.
Ptolemy VII	145 B.C.
Ptolemy VIII	170–116 B.C.
Ptolemy IX	116–107 B.C.
Ptolemy X	107–88 B.C.
Ptolemy XI	80 B.C.
Ptolemy XII	80–51 B.C.
Cleopatra VII	51–30 B.C.

FAMOUS PHARAOHS

THE NAMES of over one hundred pharaohs are known from inscriptions. But little is known about most of them. Much more is known about a few famous kings, like Ramses II, who covered temple walls with detailed accounts of his exploits. Royal mummies have also revealed many fascinating details.

DJOSER (REIGNED C.2650 B.C.)

The earliest known reference to the sun god Ra is on a relief celebrating Djoser's name. This powerful king led expeditions to Sinai in search of turquoise. He built the first pyramid, the Step Pyramid at Saqqara, and was buried inside.

KHUFU (CHEOPS) (2587–2564 B.C.)

Khufu built the Great Pyramid at Giza. This monumental feat must have used nearly all of Egypt's workforce for about 20 years. Its treasures were robbed long ago. But in 1925, gilded furniture from the burial of Khufu's mother was discovered.

KHAFRA (CHEPHREN) (2556–2530 B.C.)

This pharaoh was the builder of the second pyramid at Giza, which is only 13 ft (4 m) shorter than Great Pyramid. Khafra succeeded Khufu and may well have been his younger brother. Khafra's pyramid is part of a complex of buildings, which includes a well-preserved valley temple, made from massive slabs of granite. The temple housed 23 life-size statues of the king. Among these was the famous seated statue of Khafra, the falcon god Horus perched on the back of his throne. Carved from diorite, it is now in Cairo Museum. The Great Sphinx, which crouches in front of the Giza complex, is thought to be a portrait of Khafra.

MENKAURA (MYCERINUS) (2526–2506 B.C.)

He built Giza's third pyramid (the smallest). The earliest known statue of a king and queen is Menkaura arm in arm with his favorite wife.

MENTUHOTEP II (2055–2004 B.C.)

He was a Theban prince and energetic warrior. In c.2040 B.C. he became founder of the Middle Kingdom when he conquered the north and reunited Egypt. He ruled for 51 years and was buried in a great rock tomb in the cliffs at Deir el-Bahri.

SENUSRET III (1874–1855 B.C.)

This Middle Kingdom pharaoh extended royal control over Egypt's many *nomes* (districts). He also conquered part of Nubia and developed the chain of massive mud-brick forts protecting Egypt's southern border.

HATSHEPSUT (1479–1457 B.C.)

Hatshepsut was the first woman pharaoh. She married her half-brother, Thutmose II, and ruled alongside him, holding most of the power. When he died, her stepson Thutmose III took the throne. But he was still a child, so Hatshepsut ruled Egypt until her death. She pursued peaceful policies, building up the economy instead of fighting her neighbors. She opened new turquoise mines, sent a trading expedition to Punt, and erected two obelisks at Karnak. On the walls of her temple at Deir el-Bahri, she had herself portrayed as a man, with a false beard and all the other symbols of kingship.

THUTMOSE III (1479–1425 B.C.)

After his stepmother's death, Thutmose III became a powerful warrior king, extending Egyptian power deep into Asia. He added to the great temple to Amun at Karnak and erected obelisks, including *Cleopatra's Needle* – now in London.

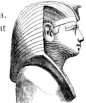

AMENHOTEP III (1390–1352 B.C.)

This pharaoh ruled a huge empire at the height of its wealth. He built the Colossi of Memnon and Luxor temple. He also added to Karnak temple. His new palace at Malkata was next to the world's first known chariot racetrack.

AKHENATEN (1352–1336 B.C.)

Crowned Amenhotep IV, the "heretic pharaoh" took a great interest in the sun god Aten. After six years as king, he changed his name to Akhenaten in the god's honor. His new religion was the first in history to worship a single god. He created a new city, Akhetaten, at Amarna. Here, art flourished in new, original styles, and lavish offerings were made to Aten. The pharaoh closed the traditional temples, depriving many priests of their power. He also ignored affairs of state, and the normally efficient Egyptian government was in chaos. When he died, his city was abandoned and his statues defaced. His wife Nefertiti may have ruled on alone.

TUTANKHAMUN (1336–1327 B.C.)

The old gods were restored under Akhenaten's successor, the boy-king Tutankhamun. His father was probably Akhenaten. Another wife, Kiya, is more likely to have been his mother than Nefertiti. For most of the pharaoh's nine-year reign, power lay with an army general (Horemheb) and an elderly official (Ay). Both went on to rule Egypt after Tutankhamun died at age 18 or 19. His mummy shows skull damage, and some experts think he may have been murdered by Ay. He would barely have been remembered at all had his intact tomb full of glittering treasures not been found in 1922.

HOREMHEB (1323–1295 B.C.)

This king was a successful army general, who took the throne after the death

of Tutankhamun's elderly successor Ay. He banned the Aten religion and set about erasing the names of "heretics" Akhenaten and Tutankhamun (born Tutankh*aten*).

SETY I
(1294–1279 B.C.)
Great war leader Sety I revived Egypt's expansion policy in the East by marching into Syria and driving back the Hittites. In 1817, his splendid Theban tomb was discovered. His well-preserved mummy is in Cairo Museum.

TAHARQO
(690–664 B.C.)
The most famous Nubian king of Egypt, Taharqo is mentioned in the Bible. He revived classic traditions in art and followed Egyptian gods. Ousted by Assyrian invaders, he was buried in a pyramid in Nubia (Sudan).

RAMSES II (1279–1213 B.C.)
Known as Ramses the Great, this king fought an indecisive battle with the Hittites, then signed the world's first official peace treaty. In the 60 peaceful years that followed, he built many monuments to celebrate his "victory." Ramses II had more than 100 children. His mummy shows that he was very tall.

CLEOPATRA VII (51–30 B.C.)
The last Ptolemaic pharaoh and the only one to speak Egyptian, Cleopatra tried to prevent Rome taking over Egypt. She had an affair with the Roman general Julius Caesar, and they had a son. After Caesar's death, she fell in love with another Roman general, Mark Antony. They had three children and planned to rule a mighty kingdom together. But they were defeated by Octavian, Antony's political rival. Octavian pursued them to Egypt, where Antony killed himself after receiving a false report of Cleopatra's death. She surrendered to Octavian. But when she could not win him over, she committed suicide – legend says, by clasping a poisonous asp (cobra) to her breast.

RAMSES III
(1184–1153 B.C.)
He saved Egypt from a series of foreign invasions and fought against corruption. Court

members, including one of his wives, tried to poison him. They were tried and forced to kill themselves. A second plot may have succeeded; he died a year later.

GODS OF ANCIENT EGYPT

DIFFERENT GODS AND GODDESSES were popular at
different times, and most changed their character
over the centuries. Here are a few of ancient Egypt's
most important deities.

KHNUM
Creator god Khnum was
worshipped as a ram or a
ram-headed man. He was
said to mold children on
a potter's wheel, then
plant them in their
mother's body.

GEB
One myth tells that the
earth god Geb and his
wife, sky goddess Nut,
created the sun, which is
reborn each day. Geb is
shown with a goose, the
hieroglyph for his name.

PTAH
The center of worship for
this god was Memphis. The
city priests maintained that
Ptah was the supreme god,
who created all the other
gods by speaking their names.

ANUBIS
Jackal-headed Anubis
was god of the dead
and mummification. He
watched over the mummy
and supervised many
funerary rites.

NEPHTHYS
This goddess was the sister
of Isis, and she helped Isis
resurrect the mutilated body
of Osiris. The two sisters
are usually shown together.
They protected coffins and
canopic jars, often in the
form of a pair of hawks.

SOBEK
This crocodile god
was ruler of the water,
and the Nile was said
to be his sweat. The
main centers of worship
were places where the
danger of crocodile
attacks was high.

ABYDOS TRIAD

Triads were small families of gods worshipped in a particular area. The family consisted of a husband, wife, and son. The Abydos triad was Osiris, his wife Isis, and their son, the sky god Horus.

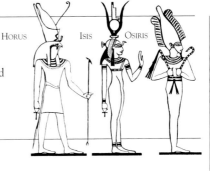

HORUS   ISIS   OSIRIS

KHONS   MUT   AMUN

THEBAN TRIAD

The chief god worshipped at the temples of Karnak and Luxor was the creator god Amun. His wife Mut was a war goddess, sometimes shown as a vulture or a lioness. Their son was Khons, a moon god, often depicted as a mummy.

FORMS OF MAAT

Many gods took various forms in different times or settings. Here are three representations of the goddess Maat, who stood for justice, truth, and order. In each of these forms, she is wearing the *Feather of Truth* on her head.

HATHOR

This goddess of the sky and of love was associated with the cow. She was often shown with horns that held the sun.

THOTH

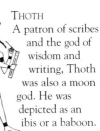

A patron of scribes and the god of wisdom and writing, Thoth was also a moon god. He was depicted as an ibis or a baboon.

HIEROGLYPHS

EGYPTIAN picture-writing is called hieroglyphs, which means "sacred symbols" in Greek. The symbols could have various meanings.

Symbol is used for these sounds

The alphabet

Every word was written exactly as it was pronounced, although only in consonants. Vowels were omitted. The alphabet consisted of 24 hieroglyphs, each representing different sounds.

Owl faces right, so read right to left

This is a weak consonant, not a vowel

READING THE RIGHT WAY
A hieroglyphic text could be read from left to right, right to left, or top to bottom. The symbols of animals or people tell you which way to read – always read toward the faces.

W MOON UNDER WICK — QUAIL CHICK	**TH** THree — COW'S BELLY	**Y,I** YOUNG INK KITE — REED LEAF
J JUNK GIN — SNAKE	**T** LOAF OF BREAD	**B** LEG
G GAP — POT STAND	**P** MAT	**TH** THAT — UNKNOWN
N WATER	**D** HAND	**M** OWL
F,V HORNED VIPER	**K** HILL	**H** TWISTED FLAX
H REED HUT	**L,R** MOUTH	**A** MAY — ARM
A,E,O VULTURE	**Z** DOOR BOLT	**CH** CHIP — TETHERING ROPE
S FOLDED CLOTH	**SH** POND	**K** BASKET

GROUP SIGNS

To save time, many hieroglyphs represent not one, but two or even three sounds together. For example, instead of spelling "sa" with two hieroglyphs, one for each of the separate sounds, it could be spelled with one symbol, a duck.

 DUCK = S+A = SA

 BEETLE = KH+P+R= KHEPER

 HOUSE = P+R = PER

 TABLE WITH BREAD = H+T+P = HOTEP

ARRANGING SYMBOLS

Symbols that made up a word did not have to be in a line; they could be fitted together in several ways, to please the eye.

 TWO WAYS TO WRITE "QUEEN"

DETERMINATIVES

Some symbols are like clues. These are determinatives. They were added to the text to make the meaning clear, but they were not read as sounds.

 PERSON   WALK, RUN   SEE   PLURAL

CLUE

Here is an example of a determinative. A scribe's pallete had two meanings. Next to a figure of a man it read "scribe," but next to a roll of papyrus it meant "to write."

FIGHTING EVIL

Egyptians thought symbols had power for good or evil. Scribes sometimes cut the heads off snakes or drew hawks with no claws to protect themselves from any harm.

GOOD LUCK
Symbols like the *Wadjet* Eye were thrown in for good luck.

EGYPTIAN NUMERALS

1 STROKE	I
10 CATTLE HOBBLE	∩
100 COIL OF ROPE	ℰ
1,000 LOTUS PLANT	
10,000 FINGER	
100,000 TADPOLE	
1,000,000 GOD SUPPORTING SKY	

The Egyptian counting system was based on the number 10, with different symbols for 1, 10, 100, etc.

Adding up the symbols gives the total.

IIIII IIII (9)

∩ IIIII III (27)

(1,200)

(54,700)

ARCHITECTURE

THE SURVIVING buildings of
ancient Egypt are mostly
religious, either temples
or tombs. Their
forms symbolize
natural cycles
and beliefs.

COLONNADE
Long colonnades were a
feature of many temples.
This one with palm-tree
capitals is from Philae.

ARTISTIC LICENCE
Some of the highly elaborate
architectural forms depicted
in tomb paintings were
obviously exaggerated.

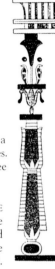

PLANT FORMS
These Old Kingdom
columns are shaped like
papyrus stems (left)
and a palm tree (right).

CARVED
Square pillars were
sculpted with figures
of gods and men, some
massive, in relief or
even in the round.
This is the god Osiris.

CAPITAL
FROM THE
TEMPLE
OF ESNA

Opening
bud

Decorated
with images
of gods

COLUMN
Temple columns could
be fluted or smooth. But
most were sculpted, often
with elaborate reliefs
that were then painted.

HIGH GATEWAY (MEDINET HABU)

Ramses III's mortuary temple and palace are enclosed within massive, 33 ft (10 m) thick walls. This ruined gateway was the main entrance to this Theban complex.

Window

KING'S HAREM

Some of rooms in the three-story gateway were used as a harem. Walls show scenes of Ramses III being attended by young women.

Detail from the painted pavement at Akhenaten's palace

FLOOR FRESCOES

The walls and floors of palaces and villas were plastered and painted with bright frescoes of patterns or nature scenes. These are from Akhenaten's palace.

AKHENATEN'S PALACE AT AMARNA

Nothing but ruined foundations of this palace remain. But it can be imagined from paintings in the tomb of high priest Meryre. This reconstructed storage area was just a small part of the vast palace complex, which was set among landscaped gardens with many trees and shady pools.

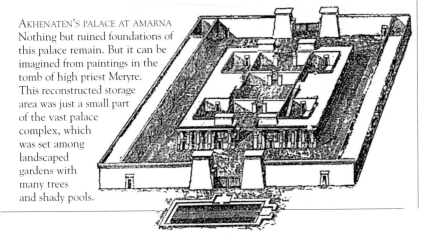

183

Glossary

AMULET
A lucky charm, worn or carried to ward off evil.

ANKH
A kind of amulet, it was the symbol of life. Only gods and kings are shown holding the ankh.

BA
A person's spirit or soul, thought to live on after death. The *Ba* is often depicted as a human-headed bird.

BOOK OF THE DEAD
A collection of up to 200 spells, placed with the mummy to help the deceased reach the other world safely.

CANOPIC JARS
Four jars used to hold the embalmed stomach, liver, lungs, and intestines.

CARNELIAN
A red semiprecious gemstone.

CARTOUCHE
A hieroglyphic symbol representing an oval-shaped loop. A pharaoh's name was written inside the cartouche.

CATARACT
A stretch of rapids that interrupt the Nile's flow.

CAUSEWAY
A raised road or path.

COLOSSUS
A larger than life-size statue, usually of a king. They are often found outside temples.

DELTA
The flat area at the mouth of a river, where the mainstream splits into marshy branches.

DEMOTIC
Developed from hieratic writing, this cursive form is found on Egyptian monuments and papyri.

DYNASTY
A succession of rulers from related families. Egypt's pharaohs formed 31 dynasties.

FAIENCE
A glazed earthenware.

FALSE DOOR
A symbolic gateway carved or painted on tombs and coffins, through which a dead person's spirit was thought to pass.

HIERATIC
A form of writing adapted from hieroglyphs. It was written on papyrus using an ink and brush.

KOHL
Black eye makeup worn by Egyptian men, women, and children.

LOWER EGYPT
The northern part of Egypt around the Nile Delta.

MUMMY
When an Egyptian died, the body was turned into a mummy. To do this, it was dried, preserved, and wrapped in linen.

MUMMY CASE
A coffin containing the mummified remains of an ancient Egyptian.

NATRON
A salt that occurs naturally in Egypt. It was used to purify and dry out the body when it was being mummified.

NECROPOLIS
A Greek word that means "city of the dead." It is used to describe Egyptian cemeteries.

NOME
A province of ancient Egypt – it was divided into areas to make government easier.

OBELISK
A tapering four-sided pillar made of stone.

OSTRACON
A flake of limestone or broken pottery that was used for writing or making rough sketches on.

PAPYRUS
A water reed used to make a kind of paper. It was the main writing material used in Egypt.

PECTORAL
A piece of jewelry that was worn on the chest.

PHARAOH
An Egyptian king. The word means "The Great House," the royal palace.

PUNT
A semimythical land that Egyptian texts refer to as a source for trade. Its exact location is still unclear, but it was south of Egypt, perhaps in Somalia.

PYLON
The monumental entrance wall of a temple.

PYRAMID
A huge tomb with a square base and four sloping sides, built to house a pharaoh when he died.

PYRAMID TEXTS
Religious writings carved on the walls inside a pyramid. They are an early version of the *Book of the Dead*, a collection of spells to help the dead pharaoh reach the next world.

RELIEF
A carved or molded sculpture that stands out from its background.

SARCOPHAGUS
A stone coffin that is either rectangular or human-shaped. The word means "flesh-eater" in Greek.

SCARAB
An Egyptian dung-beetle, symbol of rebirth.

SHABTI
From an Egyptian word meaning "to answer," this mummy-shaped figurine was placed in the tomb with a mummy. When the dead were called upon to work in the next life, they would call their *shabtis*, who they believed would answer and do the work instead.

SPHINX
A statue in the shape of a lion with the head of a man or ram. A sphinx was a symbol of royal power.

STELA
A slab of stone (or sometimes wood) with text and pictures, set up in a tomb or temple.

UPPER EGYPT
The southern part of ancient Egypt. The main city was Thebes.

URAEUS
The royal cobra, worn by the pharaoh on his brow. It was thought to spit fire at the pharaoh's enemies.

VALLEY OF THE KINGS
A desolate valley on the west bank of the Nile near Luxor, which contains the tombs of many of the New Kingdom pharaohs.

VIZIER
The chief minister. He looked after government departments responsible for running the country and reported to the pharaoh every day.

INDEX

Acknowledgments

Dorling Kindersley would like to thank:
Hilary Bird for the index; Joanne Little for
design assistance; Sarah Goulding for editorial
assistance; James Putnam for consulting on
additional material; James Anderson and
Yak El-Droubie for cartography; The British
Museum for supplying references for the
Dynasties, pages 172/173; and The
Metropolitan Museum New York for supplying
references for the hieroglyphs, pages 180/182.

Photographs by:
Peter Anderson, Geoff Brightling,
Christi Graham, Peter Hayman,
Alan Hills, Dave King, Nick Nicholls,
Kim Sayer, Ivor Kerslake, Karl Shone.

Illustrations by:
Peter Anderson, Russell Barnett,
Stephen Conlin, Peter Dennis, Dave Donkin,
Simone End, Eugene Fleury, Will Giles,
Thomas Keenes, Sandra Pond, Sarah Ponder,
Peter Visscher, J. G. Wilkinson,
John Woodcock.

Picture Credits
t top; *c* center; *a* above; *b* below; *l* left; *r* right.

The Publisher would like to thank the
following for their kind permission to
reproduce their photographs:

Ashmolean Museum, Oxford 43cra,cr,crb,
58trr;/The Griffith Institute 123tl,ca,cr; Bolton
Museum, 2br, 3tr, 12br, 23tr, 27tl, 28b, 86/7,
99br, 105tr, 111cr, 117c; Bridgeman Art
Library 61br, 72/3br;/Louvre, Paris 54bl;/The
British Museum 66cr; The British Library/
Laurence Pordes 14cr; The British Museum 1c,
2tl, tr, bl, 3l, br, 5t, 7br, 11r, 12bl, 13cb, 14b,
15tl,cl, 16tr,c,bl, 17b, 20tr, 20/21b, 21br, 27tc,
29tl,tr,cr, 30tr,b, 31tl,c,br, 32cl,clb, 34bl,
35br,tc, 37bc,tl, 38/39tc, 44/45b, 44tl,cr,
45tr,c,tl, 46/47bl, 47tl, 49bc, 50br, 54cr, 55c,
56bl, 57r,c,cl, 58cb, bl,tl, 59tl,r,bl,bc, 60br, 61tl,
62/3c, 68tl, c,br, 69tr,cla,br, 71t, 74tl,bl,
75tl,c,br, 78cr, 79br,bl, 80c, 81t,ca, 82c,cl,cr,
83tr,bl,crb,cr, 91tr, 92tl, 93br, 94tr, 95cl,c,
96/97, 98bl,r, 99tl, 101l,tr,, 102tl, 103tr, 104tr,
105bc, br,tc,cl, 107tr, 108/9tc, 108bl,br, 109bl,
110l, 112tl,cl,br,bl, 113tl,cr,bc,br,tr, 114tr,b,
115cr, 116tr,bl,cl, 117b,tl, 118cl, 119tl,ca,tr,bl,
126/7b, 127tl,tr, 129tl, 130l,cr,bc; Cairo Museum
18bl,br; Lester Cheeseman 22cr, 129r; Peter
Clayton 55br, 123bc; Robert Harding Picture
Library 100bl; Michael Holford 100cl, 103c;
The Manchester Museum (jacket), 17tl,tc,tr,
22bl, 29b, 35cr,tl, 53tr, 54bc, 55tl,tr, 66/67bc,
67cr, 78tl,cl,bl, 79ca, 82tl, 90tr,cl,cr, 91cl, cr,br,
99cl, 100tr, 103tc, 104bl,bc, 106tr,cra,bl,
106/107bc, 107br, 109br, 110cr, 111tl,
115tl,tr,br, 116br, 118br,l, 129c, 131tl, tr;
Metropolitan Museum New York 88/89bc;
John G. Ross 8/9, 12tr, 13tl, 14tl, 18c, 19tc,br,
20cl, 21tl, 23b, 26tl, 27r, 33tr,br, 35bc, 36br,
37cl, 38br, 39cla,br, 43b, 64/5, 72br, 83tl,
88c,tr, 92br, 93c, 94bl, cr, 95br,tr, 102br, 109tr,
110/1b, 120cr, 121tl,tr,cr, 120/1b, 122,cr,b,
123tr, 124/5, 128bl;/Rapho 32cr, 36clb;
The Science Museum 51br; Lin White 10tr,cr,
11tl, 23tl, 36tl, 37r, 39bc, 76/77, 88bl, 103br,
107tl, 111tr, 120cl, 126c, 128cr, 129bl, 131bl,
171tr,cr.

Every effort has been made to trace the
copyright holders and we apologize in
advance for any unintentional omissions.
We would be pleased to insert the appropriate
acknowledgment in any subsequent edition
of this publication.